Artists

VOLUME 1: A-K

FROM MICHELANGELO TO MAYA LIN

Artists

G. Aimée Ergas

U·X·L

AN IMPRINT OF GALE RESEARCH,
AN INTERNATIONAL THOMPSON PUBLISHING COMPANY

I(T)P

NEW YORK • LONDON • BONN • BOSTON • DETROIT • MADRID
MELBOURNE • MEXICO CITY • PARIS • SINGAPORE • TOKYO
TORONTO • WASHINGTON • ALBANY NY • BELMONT CA • CINCINNATI OH

Artists

From Michelangelo to Maya Lin

By G. Aimée Ergas

53
614

Staff

Carol DeKane Nagel, U·X·L Developmental Editor
Thomas L. Romig, U·X·L Publisher

Shanna P. Heilveil, Production Associate
Evi Seoud, Assistant Production Manager
Mary Beth Trimper, Production Director

Margaret A. Chamberlain, Permissions Associate (Pictures)

Pamela A. E. Galbreath, Art Director
Cynthia Baldwin, Product Design Manager

Cover Artwork: Leonardo da Vinci's *La Gioconda* (*Mona Lisa*; front left) reproduced by permission of Alinari/Art Resource; Andy Warhol portrait (front right) and Henry Moore's *King and Queen* (back left) reproduced by permission of Archive Photos/Express Newspapers.

 ™ This book is printed on acid-free paper that meets the minimum requirements of American National Standard for Information Sciences—Permanence Paper for Printed Library Materials, ANSI Z39.48-1984.

ISBN 0-8103-9862-1 (Set)

ISBN 0-8103-9863-X (Volume 1: A-K)
ISBN 0-8103-9864-8 (Volume 2: L-Z)

Printed in the United States of America

IP™ U·X·L is an imprint of Gale Research,
an International Thomson Publishing Company.
ITP logo is a trademark under license

*To my loving husband and children,
who were very patient
with not being the center of my attention
during the creation of this work.*

Contents

Salvador Dali

VOLUME 2: L-Z

Artists by Fields and Media

Bold numerals indicate volume numbers.

Alexander Calder

Architecture

Book and Magazine Illustration

Cartoons

Ceramics

Cloth and Textiles

Engraving

Environmental Art

Etching

Painting

Paper cutouts

Photography

Silk Screen

Stained Glass

Theatrical Costume Design

Theatrical Set Design

Watercolor

Wrap Art

Reader's Guide

Frida Kahlo

A rtists: *From Michelangelo to Maya Lin* presents the life
stories of 62 sculptors, painters, architects, photographers, illustrators, and designers whose works and ideas
have changed the face of art. Concentrating on North American
and European artists from the Renaissance to the modern day,
Artists provides a view of the artists' worlds—their personal
experiences and motivations and the social and artistic climates
that informed their works—and the impact of their art on society and on future generations of artists.

Format

The 62 biographies of Artists are arranged alphabetically over
two volumes. Each five- to ten-page entry opens with a portrait
of the artist, birth and death information, and a quote by or about
the artist. Accompanying several biographies are boxed sidebar
pieces discussing important movements, events, or processes,
such as impressionism, the famous Armory Show of 1913, and

how sculpture is made. In addition to the 62 artists' portraits, nearly 140 works illustrate the text.

Each volume begins with a listing of the artists featured in the set by the fields in which they worked and their favored media, a time line showing a work by each artist alongside major historical events, and a glossary of key art terms, which appear in the text in boldface the first time they are used in an entry. The volumes conclude with a list of works for further reading and a cumulative subject index providing easy access to the people, movements, and works mentioned throughout *Artists*.

Comments and Suggestions

We welcome your comments on this work as well as your suggestions for individuals to be featured in future editions of *Artists: From Michelangelo to Maya Lin*. Please write: Author, *Artists,* U•X•L, 835 Penobscot Bldg., Detroit, Michigan 48226-4094; call toll-free: 1-800-877-4253; or fax 1-313-877-4253.

Words to Know

Henry O. Tanner

Abstract art: An art style in which the subject is not represented in a naturally recognizable manner. Instead of presenting the real appearance of the subject, abstract artists try to express ideas or feelings about the subject through the use of shapes, colors, lines, and other elements. **Wassily Kandinsky** (see entry) is credited with creating the first totally abstract painting. Although abstract art is primarily a modern style, there are elements of abstraction in ancient art, especially in the use of decorative patterns.

Abstract Expressionism: A movement of **abstract art** that emerged in New York City during the 1940s and reached its peak in the 1950s. Although abstract expressionists painted in many different styles, they had in common an interest in using paint to show their emotions. They often used thick and sometimes violent brush strokes to create dense textures on large canvases. These artists considered the actions involved in the creation of a painting—including the mistakes made in the process—to be as important as the finished work. Some important artists in this highly influential movement were **Jackson Pollock** (see entry), Mark Rothko, and Hans Hoffman.

Academic art: A term used to describe art that obeyed rules set down by the important art academy or school of the day. For example, in nineteenth-century Paris the most successful artists were those who painted in the style approved by the French Academy of Fine Arts, whose standards of beauty derived from ancient Greek and Roman culture. More adventurous artists used this term in a negative manner to describe art they felt was dull and uninventive. See also **Salon.**

Avante-garde: From a French word meaning "vanguard" or "ahead of its time." When applied to art, avant-garde describes creations that are progressive, innovative, or experimental. Since it challenges established styles, avant-garde work is often controversial.

Baroque: An art style developed in the early 1600s and lasting into the early 1700s. The main characteristic of this style is its sense of unity among the arts of painting, architecture, and sculpture. Reacting against the classical and sometimes severe style of **Renaissance** art, baroque artists sought to make their works more lively and emotional. With an emphasis on bright colors, light, and exaggerated forms, many Baroque compositions exhibit a feeling of energy and movement. Baroque style later developed into **rococo** art. Notable baroque artists include **Rembrandt van Rijn, Peter Paul Rubens,** and **Diego Velazquez** (see entries).

Collage: From a French word meaning "gluing" or "pasting." A collage is an artistic composition created when such unrelated materials as cloth, newspaper, wallpaper, string, and wire are combined and pasted on a painted or unpainted surface. **Pablo Picasso** (see entry) was one of the first modern artists to use this technique. See also **photocollage.**

Color field painting: A painting style that emphasizes color as its only element. Most color field works are created on large canvases. Combining skilled technique with a sharp sense of color, artists in this style produce works that give the illusion of depth and light. From the mid-1950s to the mid-1960s, **Helen Frankenthaler** (see entry), Morris Louis, and Kenneth Noland were prominent color field artists.

Cubism: An art movement begun in the early 1900s by **Pablo Picasso** (see entry) and Georges Braque. Cubist artists abandoned the desire to render a subject with mood and emotion. Instead, they presented it broken apart into geometric shapes. In this way, they depicted the subject from several points of view at once—an attempt to portray the subject not as the eye sees it but as the mind perceives it. Cubism was one of the most important developments in modern art.

Dadaism: A literary and art movement that began in Switzerland in 1916 and lasted until 1922. Disillusioned by the effects of World War I, dada artists fought against traditional artistic values, creating art that showed absurd, nonsensical, and violent aspects of life. Some prominent dada artists were **Marcel Duchamp, Man Ray** (see entries), and Hans Arp.

Engraving: A method of printmaking whereby lines and grooves are cut with a sharp tool into a metal plate (or in some instance a wood block) and then filled with ink. After the surface of the plate is wiped clean, the plate is pressed against absorbent paper, producing an image from the pooled ink. Engravings can be original works by an artist or a way of copying an existing work. See also **etching** and **woodcut.**

Environmental art: Art that makes use of elements of natural or urban surroundings, including light, landscape, architecture, and sound, as part of the artistic creation. These works often take up large areas of space, such as city plazas or open fields. Forces of nature—like rain and sunlight—also play an important role in the effect and interpretation of the composition. Most environmental art works are temporary; photography and video are used to document the works. **Christo** (see entry) is the best-known environmental artist of our time.

Etching: A method of **engraving** that uses a metal plate covered with a layer of acid-resistant wax. The artist draws through the wax with a sharp instrument to reveal portions of the metal plate. Next the plate is dipped in acid, which attacks only the parts where the wax has been scraped away. The plate is covered with ink, then the surface is wiped clean. Afterward, paper is pressed onto the inked plate. The etched portion of the plate, which retains the ink, reveals the artist's drawing. An etching may be printed several times.

Expressionism: A term used to describe art in which the personal feeling of the artist is the most important aspect of the work. Instead of imitating real life, expressionist artists transform it to fit their creative visions. Colors, shapes, and textures are often exaggerated to show emotion. The art of **Vincent van Gogh** (see entry) is a well-known example of expressionism. Expressionist styles often have a descriptive word to identify them more specifically, such as **abstract expressionism** or German expressionism.

Fauvism: A brief art movement begun by **Henri Matisse** (see entry) and other artists in the early twentieth century. They were interested in using only pure, strong colors to define structure, to generate light, and to capture emotion in their paintings. Because the use of color in the resulting works seemed violent and uncontrolled, critics called these artists "fauves," which means "wild beasts" in French.

Folk art: The traditional art of the native inhabitants of a region whose artists have not received any formal artistic training. Many professional artists have used ideas from folk art in their works.

Fresco: From the Italian word for "fresh." A fresco is a wall painting made with pigments, the powdery substances used to make paint. The pigments are mixed with water and applied quickly to a plastered wall while the plaster is still wet. As the plaster dries, the pigment colors are absorbed into the plaster, retaining their bright hues. This technique was perfected during the Italian **Renaissance**, especially by **Michelangelo**. Fresco painting declined until the modern era, when **Diego Rivera** (see entries) sparked a renewed interest in the technique.

Impressionism: The most important movement in European art in the late 1800s. Impressionist artists, who were mostly French, explored new theories about light and color. Rather than copying a scene exactly as it looked, they used these theories to capture the "impression" of a scene as they viewed it. They were interested in the ways atmosphere and light changed the way things appeared in nature. Many styles of modern art developed from the ideas of the impressionists. Some important impressionist painters were **Claude Monet, Pierre-Auguste Renoir, Edouard Manet** (see entries), and Edgar Degas.

Kinetic art: A term describing sculpture that includes motion as a distinctive element of the work. The kinetic sculptures of **Alexander Calder** (see entry), called mobiles, are among the earliest kinetic art works.

Lithograph: A print made by drawing with a special grease crayon on a porous stone or on a grained metal plate. When water is applied to the stone or plate and ink is rolled across it, the water does not stick to the crayoned areas, but the ink does. Paper is then pressed onto the stone or plate and the retained ink prints the drawing. A lithograph can be printed several times.

Mosaic: A design made by setting small pieces of colored glass, stone, tile, wood, or other material in cement. Mosaics are often used to decorate floors or walls.

Mural: A large painting on a wall or attached to a wall. A **fresco** is one type of mural.

Op art: Short for optical art, this style became popular in the 1960s when op artists began using bright colors and intricate patterns to create illusions of movement and other effects to fool a viewer's eyes.

Perspective: A method used by artists to create the illusion of depth on a flat surface or in relief sculpture. Artists use perspective to show an object in the distance or to show the relation among objects of various sizes. Perspective was an important element of **Renaissance** art; **Leonardo da Vinci** (see entry) studied and perfected the rules of perspective drawing.

Photocollage: Also known as photomontage, a photocollage is made by combining parts of unrelated photographs into a singular composition.

Pointillism: A method of painting whereby an artist places separate, small dots of pure color side by side on a canvas. The result is such that the viewer's eyes naturally combine the colors to produce the illusion of brighter or more varied colors than if the paints had been mixed. This method was developed by late-nineteenth-century French painter **Georges Seurat** (see entry).

Pop art: An art style that emerged in England in the late 1950s as a reaction against the seriousness of **abstract expressionism** and peaked in the 1960s with the works of **Andy Warhol** and **Roy Lichtenstein** (see entries). In an attempt to marry popular culture and high art, pop artists used such images as cartoons, advertisements, movie stars, rock singers, and consumer items in their often humorous works.

Realism: A mid-nineteenth-century art style whose followers attempted to depict objects and scenes as they existed in real life, without any attempt to make them perfect or ideal. Realist artists focused on scenes of everyday life (most often the "ugly" or commonplace) rather than on biblical or heroic subjects or characters. See also **social realism**.

Renaissance: From a French word meaning "rebirth." The Renaissance was a period of heightened artistic and intellectual activity prompted by a renewed interest in the art and literature of the ancient Greeks and Romans. It began in Italy in the late 1300s and spread through Europe by the 1600s. During the Renaissance, great advances were made in areas such as science and exploration, music, literature, and the visual arts. **Michelangelo** and **Leonardo da Vinci** (see entries) were two significant Renaissance artists.

Rococo: A decorative style of art and architecture that began in eighteenth-century France and rapidly spread across Europe. A reaction to the heaviness of **baroque** decoration, the rococo is marked by delicacy and light and common motifs include shells, scrolls, leaves, and other curving shapes.

Salon: An annual exhibition of art works selected by jury and sponsored by the French Academy of Fine Arts beginning in 1737. Until the mid-nineteenth century, when the juries began to favor conservative, established art styles, it was considered a great honor for an artist's work to be exhibited in one of these influential shows. See also **academic art**.

Social realism: A form of **realism** embraced by American artists of the 1920s and 1930s who wanted to use their art to make political and economic statements about society. These artists usually depicted the lives of workers, the poor, and the homeless. Social realism is not defined by one particular artistic style but by subject content. For instance, both **Jacob Lawrence** and **Diego Rivera** (see entries) are social realists.

Still life: A work of art whose subject is inanimate objects such as flowers, fruits and vegetables, pottery, tableware, and other decorative pieces.

Surrealism: A literary and art movement founded by writer André Breton in Paris in 1924 and practiced internationally into the 1930s. It was grounded in the psychoanalytic theories of Sigmund Freud, particularly those relating to the expression of the imagination as revealed in dreams. Using a range of styles, the surrealists, such as **Salvador Dali** (see entry) and René Magritte, filled their works with fantastic imagery and dream-inspired symbols.

Woodcut: Also known as a woodblock print, a woodcut is a print made from designs cut in relief on wood. The area that is not to be printed as part of the design is carved away. Ink is then rolled on the remaining surface area and paper is applied to the block to produce the desired print. **Albrecht Dürer** (see entry) was a master of the woodblock print, the oldest method of printmaking. The designs of Japanese woodblock prints exhibited in Paris in the late nineteenth century inspired many of the impressionist painters.

Events in Art and History

Vietnam Veterans Memorial by Maya Lin

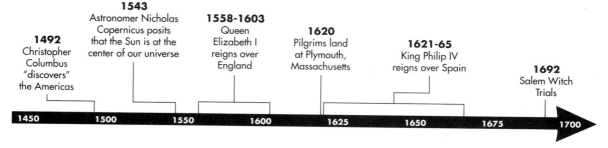

1492
Christopher Columbus "discovers" the Americas

1543
Astronomer Nicholas Copernicus posits that the Sun is at the center of our universe

1558-1603
Queen Elizabeth I reigns over England

1620
Pilgrims land at Plymouth, Massachusetts

1621-65
King Philip IV reigns over Spain

1692
Salem Witch Trials

| 1450 | 1500 | 1550 | 1600 | 1625 | 1650 | 1675 | 1700 |

xxxiii

1642 Rembrandt van Rijn, *The Night Watch*

1656 Diego Velazquez, *Las Meninas* (*Maids of Honor*)

1814 Francisco Goya, *Tres de Mayo, 1808* (*The Third of May, 1808*)

1842 J. M. W. Turner, *Snowstorm: Steamer off a Harbour's Mouth*

1863 Edouard Manet, *Le Déjeuner sur l'herbe* (*Luncheon on the Grass*)

1872 Claude Monet, *Impression: Sunrise*

1876 Pierre-Auguste Renoir, *Le Moulin de la Galette*

1880 Auguste Rodin, *The Thinker*

1884-1926 Antonio Gaudi, Church of the Sagrada Familia, Barcelona, Spain

1885 Georges Seurat, *A Sunday Afternoon on the Island of La Grand Jatte*

1886 Mary Cassatt, *Girl Arranging Her Hair*

1889 Vincent van Gogh, *The Starry Night*

1893 Henry O. Tanner, *The Banjo Lesson*

1893-95 Henri de Toulouse-Lautrec, *At the Moulin Rouge*

1897 Paul Gauguin, *Where Do We Come From? What Are We? Where Are We Going?*

1898 Paul Cézanne, *Mont Sainte-Victoire from Bibemus Quarry*

1907 Pablo Picasso, *Les Demoiselles d'Avignon*

1907 Alfred Stieglitz, *The Steerage*

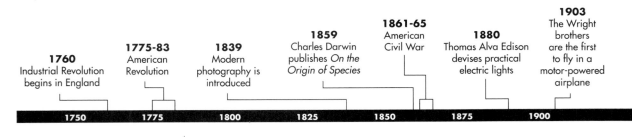

1760 Industrial Revolution begins in England

1775-83 American Revolution

1839 Modern photography is introduced

1859 Charles Darwin publishes *On the Origin of Species*

1861-65 American Civil War

1880 Thomas Alva Edison devises practical electric lights

1903 The Wright brothers are the first to fly in a motor-powered airplane

1750   1775   1800   1825   1850   1875   1900

Events in Art and History   xxxiv

1908 Henri Matisse, *Harmony in Red*

1911 Marc Chagall, *I and the Village*

1912 Marcel Duchamp, *Nude Descending a Staircase, No. 2*

1913 Wassily Kandinsky, *Improvisation 30 (Cannons)*

1921 Stuart Davis, *Lucky Strike*

1923 Man Ray, *Violon d'Ingres*

1925 Kathe Kollwitz, *Bread!*

1925-26 Walter Gropius, Bauhaus, Dessau, Germany

1927 Ansel Adams, *Monolith—The Face of Half Dome,
Yosemite National Park, California, 1927*

1928 Constantin Brancusi, *Bird in Space*

1928-29 Diego Rivera, *The Struggle of the Classes*

1929 Augusta Savage, *Gamin*

1931 Salvador Dali, *Persistence de la mémoire
(The Persistence of Memory)*

1931 Georgia O'Keeffe, *Cow's Skull: Red, White, and Blue*

1932 Berenice Abbott, *Nightview, New York, 1932*

1934 Alexander Calder, *Calderberry Bush*

1936 Frida Kahlo, *My Grandparents, My Parents and I*

1936-39 Frank Lloyd Wright, Fallingwater, the Kaufmann
House, Bear Run, Pennsylvania

1938 Henri Cartier-Bresson, *Banks of the Marne*

1941 Jacob Lawrence, *And the Migrants Kept Coming*

1942 Edward Hopper, *Nighthawks*

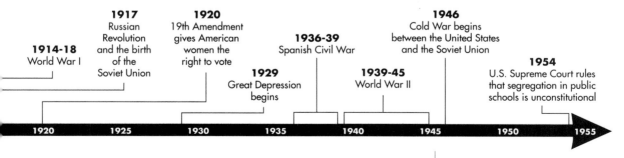

1914-18 World War I

1917 Russian Revolution and the birth of the Soviet Union

1920 19th Amendment gives American women the right to vote

1929 Great Depression begins

1936-39 Spanish Civil War

1939-45 World War II

1946 Cold War begins between the United States and the Soviet Union

1954 U.S. Supreme Court rules that segregation in public schools is unconstitutional

1920   1925   1930   1935   1940   1945   1950   1955

Events in Art and History

1942 Piet Mondrian, *Broadway Boogie-Woogie*

1950 Jackson Pollock, *Lavender Mist: Number 1, 1950*

1951-52 Isamu Noguchi, *Mu*

1952 Helen Frankenthaler, *Mountains and Sea*

1957-58 Henry Moore, *UNESCO Reclining Figure*

1961 Andy Warhol, *32 Soup Cans*

1962 Roy Lichtenstein, *Blam!*

1964 Romare Bearden, *Projections*

1967 David Hockney, *A Bigger Splash*

1970 Duane Hanson, *Tourists*

1979 Judy Chicago, *The Dinner Party*

1980 Maya Lin, *Vietnam Veterans Memorial*

1986 Faith Ringgold, *Harlem Renaissance Party*

1989-93 I. M. Pei, Le Grande Louvre, Paris, France

1992 Annie Leibovitz, *Demi Moore*

1995 Christo, *Wrapped Reichstag, Project for Berlin*

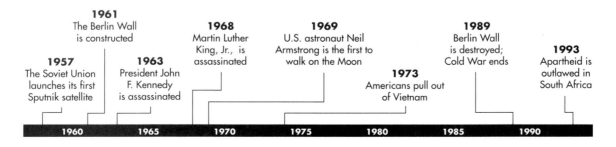

1961
The Berlin Wall
is constructed

1957
The Soviet Union
launches its first
Sputnik satellite

1963
President John
F. Kennedy
is assassinated

1968
Martin Luther
King, Jr., is
assassinated

1969
U.S. astronaut Neil
Armstrong is the first to
walk on the Moon

1973
Americans pull out
of Vietnam

1989
Berlin Wall
is destroyed;
Cold War ends

1993
Apartheid is
outlawed in
South Africa

1960   1965   1970   1975   1980   1985   1990

Artists

Berenice Abbott

Born July 17, 1898
Springfield, Ohio
Died December 10, 1991
Monson, Maine

B erenice Abbott's work spanned more than 50 years of the twentieth century. At a time when "career women" were not only unconventional but controversial, she established herself as one of the nation's most gifted photographers. Her work is often divided into four categories: portraits of celebrated residents of 1920s Paris; a 1930s documentary history of New York City; photographic explorations of scientific subjects from the 1950s and 1960s; and a lifelong promotion of the work of French photographer Eugène Atget. As a woman and a serious artist, Abbott faced numerous obstacles, not least of which was denial of the recognition she was due. Only recently has the high quality of her work been adequately appreciated. As one writer put it, "She was a consummate professional and artist."

Bernice Abbott was born into a world of rigid social rules, especially for women, who were expected to accept without question certain cultural dictates about clothing, manners, proper education, and other areas of everyday life. Abbott was an inde-

"I was glad to give up sculpture. Photography was much more interesting."

Berenice Abbott

pendent and somewhat defiant girl who hated such arbitrary constraints. One of her earliest acts of "rebellion" was to change the spelling of her name; Bernice became Berenice. "I put in another letter," she told an interviewer, "made it sound better."

Abbott's childhood was not especially happy. Her parents divorced when she was young, and though Abbott remained with her mother, her brothers were sent to live with their father. She never saw them again. This was a severe blow and may partly explain why Abbott never married or had her own family. She said she never wed because "marriage is the finish for women who want to work," and in her era this was largely true.

"Reinvented" herself in New York

At age 20 Abbott headed for New York City to "reinvent" herself, as one writer put it. She rented an apartment, studied journalism, drawing, and sculpture, and formed a circle of friends, many of whom were "bohemians" rebelling against the strict social rules of the day. Friends who remembered her from those days said Abbott was shy and "looked sort of forbidding." After three years Abbott had had her fill of New York and decided to go to Paris, something unmarried young women rarely did by themselves. In fact, that such a move was sure to generate controversy probably contributed to Abbott's decision to pursue it.

In Paris Abbott studied sculpture, but she ultimately found it unsatisfying. In 1923 photographer **Man Ray** (see entry), whom she had known in New York, offered her a job as his assistant. Abbott knew nothing about photography but accepted the job. "I was glad to give up sculpture," she said. "Photography was much more interesting." She worked for Man Ray for three years, mastering photographic techniques sufficiently to earn commissions of her own. Indeed, her work became so successful that she decided she had finally found her calling and opened her own studio.

Photographic portraits had become quite fashionable in Paris, and Abbott gained a solid reputation. She photographed

James Joyce, 1928. Reproduced by permission of ▶
Berenice Abbott/Commerce Graphics Ltd. Inc.

some of the most distinguished people of the day, including Irish writer James Joyce, French writer, artist, and filmmaker Jean Cocteau, and Princess Eugènie Murat, granddaughter of French emperor Napoleon III. Her works have been called "astonishing in their immediacy and insight," revealing much of the personality of her sitters, especially women. Abbott herself commented that Man Ray's photographs of women made them "look like pretty objects"; she instead allowed their character to come through.

Championed work of Eugène Atget

While her star was on the rise, Abbott "discovered" some pictures of Paris that she called "the most beautiful photographs ever made." She sought out the photographer, an aged, penniless man named Eugène Atget. For almost 40 years Atget had been making a poor living photographing buildings, monuments, and scenes of the city and selling the prints to artists and publishers. Abbott's keen eye detected the originality of these photos, and she befriended the old man. When Atget died in 1927, Abbott arranged to purchase all of his prints, glass slides, and negatives—more than a thousand items in all. She became obsessed with this massive collection, spending the next 40 years promoting and preserving Atget's work, arranging exhibitions, books, and sales of prints to raise money. She donated the collection to New York's Museum of Modern Art in 1968, by which time she had almost singlehandedly brought Atget from total obscurity to worldwide renown. Some critics have claimed that Abbott's devotion to Atget's works hampered her career. But she denied this, insisting, "It was my responsibility and I had to do it. I thought he was great and his work should be saved."

Abbott's career took a new turn when she returned to New York in 1929. Inspired by Atget's work and by the excitement she felt in the air, she began a new project: photographing the city as no one ever had. She spent most of the 1930s lugging her camera around, shooting pictures of buildings, construction sites, bill-

Nightview, New York, 1932. *Reproduced by permission of* ▶ *Berenice Abbott/Commerce Graphics Ltd. Inc.*

boards, fire escapes, and stables. Many of these sites disappeared during the 1930s as a huge construction boom in New York swept away the old buildings and mansions to make way for modern skyscrapers. Several of these photos were published in a 1939 book called *Changing New York*. In it Abbott wrote, "To make the portrait of a city is a life work and no one portrait suffices, because the city is always changing. Everything in the city is properly part of its story—its physical body of brick, stone, steel, glass, wood, its lifeblood of living, breathing men and women."

This task of documenting the city was not an easy one, especially for a woman. Abbott was "menaced by bums, heckled by suspicious crowds, and chased by policemen." Her most famous anecdote of the period came from her work in the run-down neighborhood known as the Bowery. A man asked her why a nice girl was visiting such a bad area. Abbott replied, "I'm not a nice girl. I'm a photographer." Finances presented further obstacles, and she spent her own money on the project until 1935, when the Federal Art Project of the Works Progress Administration began to sponsor her work. Until 1939 she was able to earn a salary of $35 a week and enjoyed the participation of an assistant. When funding ran out, however, she had to abandon the project.

Took on scientific community

Abbott continued working during the 1940s and 1950s, though largely outside the spotlight. She became preoccupied during this period with scientific photography, hoping to record evidence of the laws of physics and chemistry, among other phenomena. She took courses in chemistry and electricity to expand her understanding. Again her iron determination served her well.

The scientific community looked on her efforts with suspicion, both because of its skepticism about photography's usefulness and its hostility toward women who ventured into the virtually all-male enclave of science. She spent years trying to convince scientists and publishers that texts and journals could be illustrated with photographs, fighting the conventional belief that drawings were sufficient. In all, as Abbott told an interviewer, the project was a minefield of sexism: "When I wanted to do a book on electricity, most scientists ... insisted it couldn't be done. When I finally found a collaborator, his wife objected to his working with a woman.... The male lab assistants were treated with more respect than I was. You have no idea what I went through because I was a woman."

Political events rescued Abbott when the Soviet Union launched the first space satellite in 1957, initiating the "space race." The U.S. government began a new push in the field of science. In 1958 Abbott was invited to join the Massachusetts Institute of Technology's Physical Science Study Committee, which was charged with the task of improving high school science education. At last Abbott was vindicated in her insistence on the value of photography to science. Her biographer, Hank O'Neal,

Masterworks

Photographs

1927	*Eugène Atget*
1928	*James Joyce*
1932	*Nightview, New York*
1933	*Railroad Yards*
1935	*Iron Filings Bouncing Ball*

Books

1939	*Changing New York* (reprinted as *New York in the Thirties*)
1979	*The World of Atget*

has said that her scientific photos were her best work. This is a subject of some debate, but many agree that she was able to uniquely demonstrate the beauty and grace in the path of a bouncing ball, the pattern of iron filings around a magnet, or the formation of soap bubbles.

In her later years Abbott did some photography around the country, in particular documenting U.S. Route 1, a highway along the East Coast from Florida to Maine. During this project she fell in love with Maine and bought a small house in the woods of that state, where she lived for the rest of her life. As the popularity of photography grew in the 1970s and her life's work became recognized, Abbott was visited there by a string of admirers, photography students, and journalists. She became something of a legend in her own time, honored as a pioneer woman artist who conquered a male-dominated field thanks to "the vinegar of her personality and the iron of her character." But perhaps most importantly, students of the medium recognized the talent and artistry behind Abbot's work, among which reside some of the prize gems of twentieth-century photography.

Ansel Adams

Born February 20, 1902
San Francisco, California

Died April 22, 1984
Carmel, California

"The creative artist is constantly roving the worlds without, and creating new worlds within."

▲ **Portrait:** *Reproduced by permission of AP/Wide World Photos.*

A nsel Adams was one of the most popular and celebrated photographers of the twentieth century. His photographs of majestic mountains and the grandeur of the American West are among the most recognizable in the world. During his long career, Adams was renowned for his artistry and for developing innovative camera techniques. He used his skills as a photographer, writer, teacher, and organizer to promote his love of photography. Adams was also a strong advocate for the environment; he put his pictures to work convincing people that the beauty he photographed was a national treasure in danger of being destroyed.

Ansel Easton Adams was born to an affluent family in San Francisco. His father, Charles Hitchcock Adams, also born in San Francisco, made his living from his family's prosperous lumber business. Ansel Adams's mother, Olive Bray Adams, grew up in Carson City, Nevada. Her family home was a social and cultural center for the wealthy families of Carson City. When Adams was a baby, his parents built a new home overlooking the Golden Gate, the narrow passage connecting San Francisco Bay to the Pacific

Ocean. There was no bridge over the passage then. Adams spent much of his childhood looking out over the ocean and playing on the beach. These experiences were at the root of his love and appreciation of nature.

Preferred the outdoors to school

When Adams was four years old, his life was immeasurably disrupted by the Great San Francisco Earthquake of 1906. The family's house was almost destroyed. In his autobiography Adams recalls his memories of the quake, the fires that followed, and the fear and confusion that reigned throughout the city. But despite this traumatic experience, Adams enjoyed a happy childhood. He was a very bright and active child, though he found it difficult to concentrate and behave in school. He believed that he had what is now called a "hyperactive" condition, or an "attention deficit disorder." He was usually bored at school and preferred to be outdoors collecting insects, roller skating, or playing golf.

After a few unproductive years in a variety of schools, Adams began a course of home study, presided over by his father. Adams credited his father's patience, creativity, and positive attitude for the direction that his life would take. In 1915, when Adams was 13, his father gave him a year's pass to the Panama-Pacific International Exposition in San Francisco, a huge fair with exhibits and displays from around the world. He continued studying literature and music at home but spent most of each day at the fair learning whatever he could. He attended concerts, took in exhibitions of painting and sculpture, and visited displays of modern technology and industrial works. A friend of Adams's father managed the exhibition of a large adding machine company. He taught the boy how to use the machine, and Adams spent many hours demonstrating it to passersby. He had a great many adventures at the fair that year.

Piano his first love

Adams began studying the piano when he was about 12. He demonstrated quite a bit of talent. The discipline demanded by his teachers and the chance for self-expression provided by the music began to transform him from a "hyperactive Sloppy Joe" into a serious student. Throughout his teens and twenties, Adams studied, performed, and eventually taught piano. For many years he thought music would be his career.

In 1916, while on a family vacation to Yosemite National Park, Adams shot his first photographs with a Brownie box camera his parents had given him. He fell in love with Yosemite and returned there every summer for many years. In 1920 he landed a job as caretaker of one of the park's lodges, which was owned by the Sierra Club. (Adams would one day became director of the Sierra Club, serving for 37 years.) Each summer he took photographs; he spent the winter making photo diaries of the many wilderness trips he took into the park. As Adams's interest in photography grew, a family friend who owned a photo finishing business showed him how to develop his own prints. This friend also hired Adams to work in his darkroom.

On some of his wilderness trips, Adams dragged along a huge, 40-pound view camera, tripod, glass plates, and filters. It became more and more important to him to fully capture the feelings inspired in him by the spectacular scenery. He longed to express the excitement he felt in absorbing the quality of light and shadow, the texture, and the size of the cliffs, mountaintops, and valleys. By 1927, when he took his famous photo of the Half Dome cliff in Yosemite, he had finally begun to feel that he was using the camera as more than just a tool. Adams began to formulate his ideas about "previsualization," or the photographers process of creating an image in his or her mind and then using the camera to realize that image. Crucial to this idea was that the photographer have complete command of the techniques of photography—knowing what exposures, light, filters, and other tools would produce the desired result. Adams believed that this control must be akin to that of a musician over his or her instrument.

Early patronage and famous friends

In 1928 Adams married Virginia Best, whose father owned a music studio near Yosemite where Adams practiced piano during the summer. They enjoyed a long, happy marriage and had two children. At roughly the same time as his marriage, Adams was introduced to Albert Bender, an art collector and patron. Bender was impressed by Adams's photos and offered to publish a portfolio of his prints. This was Adams's first venture into professional photography. Bender was a tremendous influence on Adams's career and introduced him to many important artists of the time, including painter **Georgia O'Keeffe** (see entry), photographer Paul Strand, and poet Robinson Jeffers.

In 1930, after vacillating between music and photography, Adams decided that photography would be his life's work; he began to pursue it seriously, making a pilgrimage to New York City in 1933 to meet the grand patron of photography, **Alfred Stieglitz** (see entry). Stieglitz immediately grasped the genius of Adams's work and in 1936 offered him the opportunity to mount a solo show at the American Place gallery. Adams's reputation began to grow as he traveled around the United States photographing spectacular scenes of the national parks, as well as other, more remote sites. Soon the precision and pristine nature of his photographs were widely acclaimed. He also began to publish his writings and participated in numerous seminars.

During World War II Adams served as a consultant to the armed forces. He produced a photographic survey of a California internment camp in which Americans of Japanese ancestry were detained after war was declared on Japan. He published this in 1944 as *Born Free and Equal*. After the war he traveled to Alaska, Hawaii, and elsewhere to photograph national parks and monuments. He also began teaching a technique he developed called the Zone System. It allows the photographer to enhance the image photographed by judging the darkness and light on a scale from zero (black) to nine (white) and adjusting the shades of gray in between. Adams taught this system at schools and workshops around the country. Some maintain that it is his greatest contribution to photography.

Fierce protector of his favorite subject

Adams's love of nature remained a dominant theme throughout his life. Long before the environmental movement gained momentum, he was a vocal critic of the way people treated their natural surroundings. In 1950 he wrote of his concern that humankind was spoiling the planet and its resources—cutting down forests, overgrazing land, fouling water supplies. Adams continually used his influence through the Sierra Club and with the U.S. Park Service to help preserve threatened wilderness areas.

A great organizer, Adams was chief among promoters of creative photography. In the 1930s he and a group of friends established the f/64 Group to organize photographic exhibitions. He even owned his own gallery in San Francisco at one point. In 1940 he arranged for a large photography presentation at the Golden Gate Exposition in San Francisco. That year he was also

Adams at his home with **Moonrise, Hernandez, New Mexico, 1921,** *on December 2, 1980. Reproduced by permission of AP/Wide World Photos.*

Masterworks

1921	*Moonrise, Hernandez, New Mexico*
1927	*Monolith—The Face of Half Dome, Yosemite National Park, California*
1932	*The Golden Gate Before the Bridge, San Francisco*
1935	*High Country Crags and Moon, Sunrise, Kings Canyon National Park, California*
1942	*The Tetons and the Snake River, Grand Teton National Park, Wyoming*
1948	*Sand Dunes, Sunrise, Death Valley National Monument, California*
1950	*Point Sur, Storm, Monterey Coast, California*
1967	*Cypress and Fog, Pebble Beach, California*

one of the founders of the department of photography at the Museum of Modern Art in New York and later of the photography department at the San Francisco Art Institute. But perhaps his most rewarding administrative accomplishment was the establishment of the Friends of Photography in 1966. The Friends offer gallery space for exhibitions, publish photography books, give workshops, and bestow grants and awards to photographers.

For his part, Adams received numerous awards and honors during his lifetime. Several films have centered on him, many books have been published about him and his pictures, and his works have been seen in hundreds of exhibitions. The "brilliant clarity" of his photographs, wrote a reviewer in the *New York Times*, comes as a "result of a deep love of nature and a good eye," as well as the technical skill of a "master photographer." Adams led a rich and varied life, and his contributions to the art of photography form a legacy that will surely continue to inspire and nurture photographers for decades to come.

Romare Bearden

Born September 2, 1912
Charlotte, North Carolina
Died March 12, 1988
New York, New York

In a review of an extensive traveling exhibition of Romare Bearden's work mounted roughly three years after his death, a writer for *Time* magazine called him "one of the ... most distinguished black visual artists America has so far produced." Bearden was also a writer, poet, scholar, composer, and educator. He is perhaps best remembered for his pioneering work in collage and for his many contributions to the African American community through his art and teaching. He was exceptionally well versed in the art and literature of numerous cultures, and his work was unique and universal because he was adept at combining his many influences to create something completely new.

Romare Bearden was born in the house of his great-grandfather in Charlotte, North Carolina. His artistic talents may have come from several artist members of his father's family, including the distinguished African American painter Charles Alston. Bearden's parents, Richard and Bessye Johnson Bearden, moved the family to New York City when Bearden was about four years old. His father worked for the department of health,

"What I've attempted to do is establish a world through art in which the validity of my Negro experience could live and make its own logic."

and his mother was a correspondent for an African American newspaper. Bearden went to elementary school in New York but moved to Pittsburgh to live with his grandmother during high school. He was involved more in sports than art during that time. After graduation he even briefly played professional baseball. He entered New York University in 1931, majoring in mathematics and serving as art editor and cartoonist for the campus humor magazine. He received his degree in 1935.

Becomes social worker to support painting

The United States was beset by the Great Depression in 1935, and jobs were hard to find. Bearden decided to pursue his budding artistic skills, studying for two years at the Art Students League, an art school in New York. He took classes from George Grosz, a German **expressionist** known for his political drawings. The 1930s were a particularly active time for the art world, and Bearden was exposed to a wide range of styles, including **cubism**, futurism, **surrealism**, and **social realism**. He joined a group of African American artists who met at the studios of painters Alston and Henry Bannarn, where they exchanged ideas and theories.

Bearden soon realized that he could not earn a living through his art, so he took a job as a social worker with the New York Department of Social Services. He continued to paint in his free time. In the late 1930s Bearden produced a series of paintings on heavy brown wrapping paper, which he used because it was cheap. The paintings were about life in the southern United States; they showed Bearden experimenting with cubist and African styles.

In 1940 Bearden presented his first solo show in a studio in Harlem, the area of New York City where many African Americans lived. His career was interrupted, however, by World War II; Bearden served in the army from 1941 until May 1945. Later in 1945 Bearden mounted another solo show in the Kootz Gallery in New York, which showed his work regularly for the next five years. One of the pieces from the 1945 show was purchased by the highly regarded Museum of Modern Art. After the war

Bearden resumed his social work in order to earn a living, but he continued to paint. His style became more abstract, figures and objects rendered more according to how the artist felt about them than to how they actually appeared to the eye; line, shape, and color took on greater significance. Bearden painted a series of works based on the poetry of the Spaniard Federico García Lorca, as well as on the verse of the ancient Greek poet Homer. His efforts were included in many group shows, including one at the prestigious Whitney Museum in New York and another at the widely respected Art Institute of Chicago. Bearden's success was especially remarkable because his work was accepted in the mainstream, mostly white art world and not just among African American artists and collectors.

Intellectual development in Paris

With the 1950s came a major change in Bearden's life; he went to Paris in 1950 to study art and philosophy. During his two years there he met some of the most prominent artists of the time, including the Spaniard **Pablo Picasso** (see entry), French painters Georges Braque and Fernan Leger, and the Romanian sculptor **Constantin Brancusi** (see entry). Bearden also became involved with a group of black thinkers and writers, among them Leopold Sedar Senghor, who would later become the president of the west African nation of Senegal. Bearden was greatly influenced by this set's ideas about African culture and black consciousness. Bearden's newfound awareness of the importance of the African American experience made him question many of his values and his art; he stopped painting for roughly three years. He returned to his social work position in New York in 1951 and devoted himself to writing music. He spent some time copying the paintings of past masters, as well as a few modern artists like Picasso and the Frenchman **Henri Matisse** (see entry), but he did no original work.

In 1954 Bearden developed an interest in Chinese painting, experimenting with a variety of techniques. He also wrote a book with his friend artist Carl Holty about his involvement with Chinese art. Bearden's works were exhibited with some regularity in New York galleries during the late 1950s and early 1960s.

This was the heyday of the growing civil rights movement in the United States. In record numbers, African Americans began to embrace the ideas about which Bearden had learned in Paris. These concepts of black empowerment, in this case demands for participation in American political and economic life, as well as social justice, moved Bearden. His work of this period began to move away from **abstract art** to include more representational subjects. In 1963 an association of artists calling themselves the Spiral Group began meeting in Bearden's New York studio to discuss how they as African American artists fit into the struggle for civil rights.

Bearden proposed that the group collaborate on a project to display their sense of community and unity. He suggested a collage focusing on African American themes. This goal brought focus and purpose to Bearden's own work. From then on, collage became his most favored medium. The term *collage* comes from a French word meaning to glue or assemble. Collage first appeared in modern art with the advent of the cubists, initially Picasso. A collage combines cuttings from magazines and newspapers, photographs, fabric, colored paper, and virtually any material at the artist's disposal. Many collages are abstract, but Bearden was a master of the form; employing a variety of patterns and textures, he constructed images of buildings, people, and landscapes. He drew and painted on the pieces of the collage and also used photographs in a technique known as photomontage. These assemblages illuminate urban life, the dynamics of the family, religious rituals, death, and the beauty of nature. It is not surprising that an artist of Bearden's wide-ranging influences—European, African, African American, cubist, social realist, abstract—would be compelled to work in a variety of media, sampling as many materials as he could.

Establishes reputation with collage

Bearden's first collages were small, but in 1964 he had several photomontages enlarged into gigantic pieces called *Pro-*

◄ Pepper Jelly Lady. *National Museum of American Art, Washington, DC/Art Resource, NY. Courtesy of the estate of Romare Bearden.*

jections. These were exhibited in a group show with works by other members of the Spiral Group. Bearden continued producing large creations throughout the 1960s, often painting bright colors onto the patterns and colors of the raw materials of the collage. The subjects of his collages were usually the life and culture of African Americans, including memories of his childhood in the South and music, especially jazz. In fact, the *New York Times* attested that Bearden was "one of the first American artists to explore the relationships between painting and music." He was close to many of the great jazz musicians of the day, including bandleader and composer Duke Ellington and keyboardist-songwriter Fats Waller. Bearden's work became widely known through posters, a mural in New York City's Times Square, and covers he did for many magazines, such as *Time, Fortune,* and *TV Guide.* By 1966 he was finally able to earn a living from art alone.

In March 1971 the Museum of Modern Art mounted a major exhibition of Bearden's work. This was a great honor rarely bestowed upon living artists. The largest piece in the show was a six-part collage called *The Block.* In it Bearden combined several elements and styles to portray life on one city block in Harlem. The work was accompanied by an audiotape of gospel and blues singing, children's voices, and street sounds. The multimedia extravaganza portrayed the social realities and excitement of life in urban African America. The show traveled throughout the United States.

Bearden's involvement with African American life went beyond his artistic contributions. He served as art director of the Harlem Cultural Council beginning in 1964, spearheading efforts to bring more art to the community. In 1967 he codirected an exhibition of 150 years of African American art, the most extensive show on the subject ever presented. In the late 1960s he helped organize a nonprofit gallery in New York where minority artists could show their works. Bearden was also a writer and scholar. One of his colleagues insisted that if he had decided to become a writer, his career would have been just as

Family, 1988. National Museum of American Art, Washington, ▶ *DC/Art Resource, NY. Courtesy of the estate of Romare Bearden.*

Masterworks

1964	*Projections*
1967	*Three Folk Musicians*
1968	*Blue Interior—Morning*
1970	*Patchwork Quilt*
1980	*The Block*
1981	*Artist with Painting and Model*
1983	*Piano Lesson*
1986	*Quilting Time*

brilliant. He wrote some poetry, as well as a biography of African American artist **Henry Ossawa Tanner** (see entry) and a volume titled *Six Black Masters of American Art*. Art education was extremely important to Bearden, and he taught frequently at various universities and art schools. After his death, his wife established a trust fund in his name to aid in the education of art students.

In the 1980s Bearden focused on images of women and life in the South. The influence of Matisse can be seen in his use of both paper cutouts and vibrant colors. Like Matisse, who favored the warm climate of southern France in his later years, Bearden was inspired by the light and warmth of the tropics, spending much of this period in the Caribbean. One of Bearden's last projects was a commission from the Detroit Institute of Arts to create a large **mosaic** wall **mural**. Made of bits of vividly colored tile, the mural depicts a group of women making a quilt. Typical of Bearden's work, it features visualized memories of his Southern upbringing and key elements of African American culture, his deep love of which is deftly communicated to the viewer. Like the Mexican artist **Diego Rivera** (see entry), Bearden relished the opportunity to use a wall as his canvas, the better for all passersby to enjoy his work.

Less than a year before his death, Bearden was awarded the 1987 National Medal of Arts by President Ronald Reagan. This recognition reinforced the artist's powerful message: that people of all colors and cultures must celebrate their unique heritage—and from this learn how strongly they are connected to other cultures in the greater fabric of humankind.

Constantin Brancusi

Born February 21, 1876
Hobitza, Gorj, Romania

Died March 16, 1957
Paris, France

R omanian sculptor Constantin Brancusi became widely known during the first half of the twentieth century for his abstract, often egg-shaped, sculptures made of stone, wood, and metal. The subjects of his works were usually taken from nature—most often birds, fish, and human beings. Brancusi's simple, distinctly modern vision stemmed largely from his study of prehistoric, Oriental, and African art. In essence, he traveled through history and around the world to create a vision for the future.

Brancusi's family were peasants from the southern part of Romania. The artist left home when he was about ten years old, reportedly to follow a band of gypsies, and worked at odd jobs around the countryside. By the time he was 18, he had landed in the city of Craiova, where he studied at the School of Arts and Crafts and was assistant to a furniture maker. Here he learned the craft of finishing and polishing wood, a skill he would later use in his sculpture and sculpture bases. After four years in Craiova, Brancusi moved to Bucharest, the capital of

"Don't look for obscure formulas or mystery in my work. It is pure joy that I offer you."

▲ *Portrait: Reproduced by permission of The Bettmann Archive.*

23 | Constantin Brancusi

Romania, to study at the Academy of Fine Arts. During this early period of his career he worked within the framework of traditional sculpture, attempting to render his subjects in the most realistic manner possible. At the Academy he won first prize for a sculpture of a standing man; the piece was so detailed and exact that it was soon employed as a model of anatomy at the Bucharest medical school.

Becomes intrigued by African art

In 1904 Brancusi went to Paris. His journey there spanned two years because the sculptor walked from Bucharest. Paris was then the center of the European art world; artists of all stripes were engrossed in experiments with a host of new styles that would one day become the foundations of modern art. Brancusi held several jobs during this period and studied in the workshop of a traditional sculptor. But within three years, a handful of influences would fundamentally change Brancusi's work. Like Spanish painter **Pablo Picasso** (see entry) and many other artists, Brancusi fell under the spell of African masks and statues; he gave up modeling in clay, preferring to carve in wood and chisel in stone as the African artists had.

Another key factor in Brancusi's artistic development was the work of French sculptor **Auguste Rodin** (see entry). To Brancusi, Rodin had rescued sculpture from what he saw as the stifling neoclassicism of the nineteenth century. "Thanks to him sculpture became human again," he wrote. "The influence of Rodin was and remains immense." In fact, many who recognized Brancusi's talent tried to convince him to study with Rodin, who then was in his sixties. Brancusi declined, explaining, "Rodin accepted me as a student. But I refused because nothing grows under large trees." He feared being smothered by Rodin's artistic strength and creativity.

By 1908 Brancusi's break with tradition had surpassed even that of Rodin. He felt that his artistic adherence to the time-honored methods had reduced him to "sculpting corpses."

The Kiss, *1908. Reproduced by permission* ▶
of Giraudon/Art Resource, NY.

Bird in Space, *1928.*
Bronze (unique cast),
54" x 8½" x 6½".
The Museum of Modern
Art, New York. Given
anonymously. Photograph
© 1995 The Museum of
Modern Art, New York.

His most famous work from this time is called *The Kiss.* By carving a few simple elements into a block of limestone— just hair, eyes, and arms—Brancusi was able to suggest a man and woman kissing. The work was called "the most abstract sculpture of its period." This technique of reducing details to a bare minimum became Brancusi's trademark. One of his most common themes was birds and the nature of flight. He said he "wanted to get at the essence, or the spirit" of his subjects. He found this spirit in the most basic shapes, materials, and surfaces.

Works prized for their exquisite finish

Brancusi was a slow, careful craftsman. He sometimes spent many months polishing and refining the surface of the metal or stone he used. He also created the bases on which each sculpture was mounted. His fine rendering of these pieces was noted as much for its quality as were his artistic notions for their singularity.

Brancusi's sculptures were indeed unique. Two of them sparked significant controversy. In 1920 Brancusi presented a work called *Princess X* at a large exhibition in Paris. There was a storm of protest over this abstract "portrait." Many observers were offended by what they considered its highly sexual nature. The work was temporarily removed from the exhibit.

Another of Brancusi's creations, *Bird in Space,* was involved in a lawsuit in the late 1920s. The piece is a smooth, slender, curved form made of highly polished brass. When Brancusi sought to bring the work to the United States for an exhibition, U.S. customs officials ruled that it was not a work of art because it did not seem to represent a specific subject. They maintained that *Bird* was merely a piece of metal and as such, Brancusi would have to pay an import tax on it. The artist was forced to sue the U.S. Customs Service in order to bring the work into the country. Several well-respected artists and critics aided Brancusi in the suit, which was ultimately settled in his favor. The judge in the case ruled that even though the sculpture did not resemble a bird, it was a work of art because "of its symmetrical shape, artistic outlines, and beauty of finish."

Creates imposing *Monument for Tirgui Jui*

Brancusi's largest commission came in 1937 when he was asked to create a monument to honor those from his hometown who had fought in World War I. The result, the *Monument for Tirgui Jui*, is a group of three massive sculptures. One, *The Gate of the Kiss*, takes the shape of an arch decorated with forms relating to the earlier *Kiss*. *The Table of Silence* is a huge stone table surrounded by 12 stone stools. It is said to refer to both Christian ideas of the Last Supper and to the legend of King Arthur and the Knights of the Round Table. The third element of the monument is *The Endless Column*, a cast-iron tower 118 feet high. Brancusi left the top with an unfinished look to symbolize the link between earth and sky.

Brancusi lived in Paris during his entire adult life. He spent virtually all of his time working. He rarely went out and in his later years became something of a recluse, living alone and working unaided in his studio. The studio, behind a green fence at the end of a dead-end alley in the middle of the city, was filled with tree trunks and large blocks of stone waiting to be sculpted. Brancusi never tired of exploring the streamlined forms that were his passion; nor did he grow weary of attempting to express the beauty of the natural world through his famous egg shapes, birds, columns, and animals. He was very fond of music and in his later years became interested in Eastern religions and mysticism.

Because Brancusi was such a careful craftsman, always seeking perfection in his sculpture, historians estimate that he completed fewer than a hundred pieces during his career. What he did produce, however, appears in museums around the world. His style was so unique that one is hard pressed to

Masterworks

1906	*Sleeping Muse*
1908	*The Kiss*
1913	*Mlle. Pogany*
1916	*Princess X*
1924	*The Beginning of the World*
1928	*Bird in Space*
1930	*Fish*
1937-38	*Monument for Tirgui Jiu*

compare him to other sculptors of his generation. Despite his lack of affiliation with any established school, though, Brancusi's ideas influenced most of the important sculptors who followed him, including the Italian Amedeo Modigliani, noted for his elongated nudes and portraits, and the American **Isamu Noguchi** (see entry), who actually apprenticed with the master and many of whose sculpted forms subtly bear Brancusi's imprint.

Pieter Bruegel

*Born c. 1525
Breda, the Netherlands
Died September 1569
Brussels, Belgium*

More than any other artist, Pieter Bruegel gave later generations a picture of sixteenth-century northern European life. Bruegel's paintings and prints not only portrayed everyday life, but also commented on the political and social turmoil of the artist's times. His artistic career was short—only about 15 years—yet his works have survived thanks to their detailed and realistic portrayal of nature and people.

Although Bruegel conveyed a great deal about his era through his work, he left behind little information about his personal life. Even the date and place of his birth are uncertain. By going backward from the date he joined the master painters guild in Antwerp, Holland—1551—historians have been able to calculate his birth date. Since most artists appear to have joined the guild at age 26, the painter is estimated to have been born in roughly 1525. It is also thought that he was born in a small village, possibly named Bruegel, near the city of Breda, in the Netherlands. Historians believe that Bruegel

"Many of Bruegel's pictures offer a round-trip ticket to a 16th Century Flemish village fete."

Timothy Foote

got his early art training from a master painter named Pieter Coecke van Aelst; he later married van Aelst's daughter, Mayken. Nothing is known about his education, though his friendships with several leading scholars of the time suggest that he was certainly cultured, regardless of his formal study.

Visited Italy

After joining the painter's guild, Bruegel, like many other young painters, made a pilgrimage to Italy. He traveled for four years, mostly on foot. The great painter and sculptor **Michelangelo** (see entry), though at an advanced age, was still working then, as were other important Italian painters of the time, including **Titian** (see entry), Tintoretto, and Veronese. The **Renaissance** exercised a profound influence on many northern European artists. They usually returned home to paint in the popular classical style.

Bruegel, however, was different; though he came home from his journey full of elements of the landscapes he saw, he never adopted the Italian style of painting, which above all focused on a central scene or figure. Bruegel's uniquely recognizable style spreads the viewer's attention across his canvasses. Using rich colors and ample detail, his paintings draw viewers into a scene and stretch their imaginations around corners, into doorways, and over the next hill.

Bruegel returned from Italy in 1555. He first settled in Antwerp and worked for a printmaker named Hieronymous Cock. Cock published some of Bruegel's prints of landscape scenes in about 1556 and his most popular series of prints, "The Seven Deadly Sins" and "The Virtues," in 1558. These intricate drawings illustrate the sins of greed, anger, and pride and the virtues of patience, charity, and hope, among others.

Paintings marked by intriguing detail

Bruegel undertook his first known paintings during this period in Antwerp. In the *Netherlandish Proverbs* of 1559, Bruegel illustrated 100 sayings about human failings like deceit

and foolishness. Human figures represent these foibles; a man banging his head against a brick wall, for example, depicts futile persistence. Hundreds of tiny details make this and other Bruegel paintings endlessly fascinating.

For unknown reasons, Bruegel changed the spelling of his name around 1559. Before this it had been spelled with an "h"— Brueghel. His sons later restored the letter, though confusion nonetheless resulted over the years.

Around 1563 Bruegel moved to Brussels, set up his own studio, and was married. As he grew older, the subjects of some of his paintings became more serious. He often painted religious images in modern settings, using this device to comment on political and social turmoil—especially the suppression of Protestantism by the Spanish Catholic rulers of the Netherlands. Conflicts over political self-rule eventually led to a war for independence from Spain.

The Peasant Wedding, 1565. Panel, 44⅞" x 64⅛". Kunsthistorisches Museum, Vienna. Reproduced by permission of Foto Marburg/Art Resource, NY.

Rendered scenes of peasant life

In the mid-1560s Bruegel painted the scenes of peasant life for which he is best known. One biographer who wrote shortly after Bruegel's death claimed that the painter liked to disguise himself as a peasant to observe his subjects' lives and manners. His observations were numerous and detailed. His paintings *The Wedding Dance, The Peasant Dance,* and *The Peasant Wedding* draw the viewer into the scene, alongside the large, burly men bringing the soup to the wedding feast on a plank, while a man in the corner is pouring drinks into large mugs. In the *Peasant Dance* the piper plays a tune while two children frolic nearby and a couple embrace off to the side. Among the most detailed figures Bruegel painted are the men in his painting *The Blind Leading the Blind.* It is said that Bruegel rendered the ravages of their eye diseases with such accuracy that modern doctors have been able to diagnose each one.

Bruegel also created a series of landscapes that illustrate the months of the year. Of these works—celebrated for restoring grandeur and power to landscape painting—only five remain. The people at work and play in these landscapes are dwarfed by the overall scheme of nature. The best known of the five paintings is *Hunters in the Snow,* in which the harsh, cold environment's punishing effect on the human community conveys Bruegel's conception of the power of nature.

The last years of Bruegel's life were apparently busy ones. Twenty-five paintings still exist from those years, and the painter is known to have completed others. His fame was growing, and he received a commission from the Brussels City Council. His two sons, Pieter II (or the Younger) and Jan, were born in 1564 and 1568, respectively. They too became painters of some renown. Sadly, they were never able to study with their father, as he died when they were very young. But his legacy was passed on to them—and to us. Bruegel's work was admired by later

northern masters such as **Peter Paul Rubens** (see entry), though many art historians considered it common and coarse. Indeed, the glow of the Italian Renaissance seemed to eclipse the imaginative style of the northern master. Modern viewers, however, appreciate Bruegel's "common" subject matter and his direct, engaging style.

Hunters in the Snow, 1565. Approx. 46" x 64". Kunsthistorisches Museum, Vienna. Reproduced by permission of Foto Marburg/Art Resource, NY.

Alexander Calder

Born July 22, 1898
Lawnton (Philadelphia), Pennsylvania
Died November 11, 1976
New York, New York

"Why must art be static? The next step in sculpture is motion."

▲ *Portrait: Reproduced by permission of Archive Photos/AFP.*

Alexander Calder has been called "unquestionably one of the most original and gifted men in the entire history of American sculpture." His fascination with motion led him to create a completely new form: moving sculpture. Calder's materials—most often wire and sheet metal—were as cutting-edge as his ideas, yet his creations display a deeply human perspective. His sense of humor, warmth, and love of life are evident in the small wire performers and animals of his famous *Circus* and in his huge stabiles (abstract sculptures or constructions similar in appearance to mobiles but made to be stationary) for big-city skyscrapers. A friend and critic of the artist once attested, "Public sculpture was a stuffed-shirt's paradise until Calder came along."

Calder's choice of vocation was no doubt influenced by his family. His mother, Nanette Lederer Calder, was a painter; his father, Alexander Milne Calder, and his grandfather, Alexander Stirling Calder, were both well-known sculptors.

Moreover, most of his parents' friends were artists. At an early age Calder began making jewelry, toys, and gadgets from materials he found around the house. His family moved several times during his childhood between New York State and California; in each house he was able to set up a little workshop.

Begins career as engineer

After graduating from high school, Calder decided to become an engineer, opting to attend the Stevens Institute of Technology in New Jersey. An excellent student, Calder also impressed his peers with his pleasant nature and ability to make them laugh. He studied mechanical drawing, applied kinetics (a branch of science that deals with the effects of forces on the motions of bodies or with changes in a physical or chemical system), and descriptive geometry, unaware at the time how well this background would serve his art.

In the years immediately following his graduation, Calder held a wide variety of jobs: automotive engineer, mapmaker, machinery salesman, efficiency engineer, even crew member in the boiler room of a passenger ship. Calder wrote that several ideas for inventions occurred to him during his time in the boiler room; one was to "spew a mouthful of drinking water up into the air—it would come down with a shower effect." Calder's many occupations afforded him the opportunity to travel through much of the United States. He later returned to New York to study for several months at the Art Students League.

Early in 1924 Calder got his first art position, as a sports illustrator for the *National Police Gazette* newspaper. Using his press pass, Calder was able to spend two weeks in the spring of 1925 sketching scenes at the Ringling Brothers Barnum & Bailey Circus; thus began a lifelong fascination with the big top. Calder also held a job requiring that he decorate a sporting goods store in New York City with portraits of athletes. But it was a collection of drawings he'd done at zoos in New York that comprised his first book, *Animal Sketching,* which was published in 1926. That year the artist left New York for Paris.

Creates *Circus* in Paris

In Paris Calder took art classes and, in his tiny studio, began building his first movable wood and wire sculpture. The result was his famous miniature circus, the characters of which were based on his New York circus drawings. There were elephants, acrobats, seals, lions, and even a ringmaster, all made of wood, rubber, wire, cork, buttons, bottle caps, and fabric. Soon Calder's circus began attracting an audience. Some of the most important—and soon-to-be-important—artists of the day came to see the funny American "play with his toys." The miniature circus became a popular diversion and brought Calder in contact with the leaders of the art community in Paris.

This attention led him to experiment more seriously with wire sculpture, which he began to make on a larger scale, employing a more three-dimensional structure. Calder's wit and playfulness came through in these pieces; made of wire and sheet metal, the figures are full of spidery lines and curlicues. He gave them such whimsical titles as *Blue Elephant with Red Ears, Crested Cow,* and *The Only, Only Bird.* One of his most clever sculptures is *Umbrella Lamp,* which portrays a skinny pedestrian holding a toy umbrella; the figure's head is a light bulb. Calder occasionally brought his creations to the real animal kingdom: he once made a cigarette carton into a cow mask for his cat.

An important influence on Calder was the work of artist **Piet Mondrian** (see entry). On visiting Mondrian's studio, he expressed the wish that Mondrian's paintings could all be set in motion. Mondrian painted largely in black and white, utilizing primary colors—red, blue, and yellow—for accent. Calder adopted this color theme for most of his own works. On the rare occasion that someone wished him to use a different scheme, he protested vehemently.

In 1929 Calder presented his first solo show in Paris, displaying his wood and wire sculptures; shows in New York and Berlin followed. During the early 1930s, he traveled between New York and Paris frequently; on one of many voyages by passenger ship to New York, he met Louisa James, whom he married in 1931. As his stature grew, Calder found himself welcomed into a number of progressive art circles. He was invited to exhibit with the Abstraction-Creation group in Paris and saw his works included in an event at the prestigious Museum of Modern Art in New York.

Develops concept of kinetic art

During the 1930s and early 1940s, Calder developed the concept of sculpture that both defines and moves within the space that contains it. This idea—inspired partly by the relationships of planets, stars, and other celestial bodies—became the basis of Calder's style, later known as **kinetic art.** His first stabiles, from 1931, were stationary constructions developed from his wire sculptures. He suspended little balls or free-form shapes from long wires, suggesting a model of the solar system.

The Movement of Kinetic Art

A new kind of energy was injected into art, especially sculpture, when modern artists introduced actual movement— rather than implied motion—into their work. The term *kinetic* comes from the Greek word meaning motion; it can also mean active and lively. Of course, sculpture has tried to suggest movement throughout its history; revered French sculptor **Auguste Rodin** (see entry), for example, was fascinated by the ability of dancers to convey feeling.

But actual moving parts didn't find their way into sculpture until the modern era. It was **Marcel Duchamp** (see entry) who in 1913 attached a bicycle wheel to a stool so it could turn freely. Other artists used motors to move parts of their sculptures. And in the early 1920s, Hungarian painter, designer, and photographer Laszlo Moholy-Nagy in-troduced the movement of light into his works. Alexander Calder is probably the best known of this early generation of kinetic artists: the random movements of his mobiles brought a new conception of space to art. All these artists were products of the machine age; they combined the science of physics with human creativity.

Kinetic art contradicts the traditional idea that an artwork is static, unchanging. With the introduction of movement, forms can change and a work can alter the space around it. The viewer's perception of a piece can change even if he or she doesn't move; indeed, an artwork can transform it-self constantly and might never appear exactly the same way twice. This development complicates the idea of an art "treasure," preserved forever as the artist formed it, and even raises the potential for each piece to be forever re-created in collaboration with the viewer. This was as impor-

The next year Calder began creating mobiles, moving sculptures that hung from ceilings or were suspended from large bases. He experimented continually with weight balance in order to convey graceful, natural movement. He first tried to power his mobiles with small motors but disliked their predictable, steady motion. Calder found the random and unexpected movement caused by wind or air currents in a room much more interesting. His constructions based on random motion, in contrast to the frozen moment captured in traditional sculpture, represented a considerable innovation. With the unique combination of his engineering expertise and spirit of creative exploration, Calder

tant a revolution for sculpture as **cubism** was for painting.

The 1950s saw a flowering of interest in kinetic art. The availability of new materials and technology gave rise to previously unimagined possibilities. Light and sound were added to the element of motion. A large exhibit in 1955 in Paris brought together the kinetic works of Duchamp, Calder, Victor Vasarely, Jean Tinguely, Yaacov Agam, and many others. The exhibit demonstrated how the popularity of both photography and the automobile had helped create the desire for motion in art.

A worldwide movement grew throughout the 1960s. Artists like Nicolas Shoffer worked with cybernetics, the theory of computer systems and communications. He created settings of light and motion for ballets and large outdoor spectacles. Motorized robots, vibrating metal strips, rolling balls, and magnetized metal shavings were integrated into sculpture. The neon light tube became a favorite tool of artists during the decade.

The space age also figured prominently in the concepts and materials artists used. Several noted artists led "double lives" as engineers, chemists, or doctors. Scientist Frank Joseph Malina was prominent in the development of the U.S. rocket program. Beginning in the 1950s, he spent more and more time creating works of art, employing transparencies, colored threads, artificial light, and small motors as media.

Much of the work of kinetic artists overlapped and combined with another trend in art called optical art or **op art**. With the dawn of these schools, the traditional divisions between painting, sculpture, dance, music, and other arts had begun to disappear; more than ever, the means for defining a work of art were thrown into question.

had helped modernize the art of sculpture. By the end of the 1930s, the general form of Calder's mobiles and stabiles had been established. These works often have the names of animals— *Spider, Whale, Black Beast.* The stabiles are broad, usually curved structures planted on the ground; they often resemble huge spiders or dinosaurs.

Eventually Calder and his wife bought a farmhouse in Connecticut. His studio there looked like a factory, with wires, poles, sheet metal, tools, and crates everywhere. During this period, interest in the artist's work began to grow. Calder's kinetic sculpture was displayed frequently in the United States and Europe

throughout the 1930s and 1940s. In a catalogue for a 1946 Calder exhibition, the French writer and philosopher Jean-Paul Sartre wrote, "When everything goes right a mobile is a piece of poetry that dances with the joy of life and surprises."

Posters, ballet, airplanes, and race cars

In 1943 the Museum of Modern Art installed a large exhibition of Calder's work that included performances of *Circus* by the sculptor himself. It was a huge success. Commissions poured in from governments, businesses, and private citizens all over the world—and not just for his sculptures: Calder designed posters and prints, rugs and tapestries. He made jewelry, designed sets and costumes for theatrical productions and ballets, illustrated books, and created toys for his children and grandchildren. He also drew and painted with oils. In the 1970s Braniff Airlines commissioned Calder to paint some of their jets with his designs, a particularly fitting request given his love of movement. He also decorated a racing car for the BMW motor company. "What he wanted to work, worked," attested his friend *New York Times* art critic John Russell.

The Calder family, including two daughters, bought a house near Tours in central France in 1953. This became their principal home and later Calder's main studio, though he kept his home in Connecticut. His reputation continued to grow, and by the 1960s Calder had emerged as one of the most celebrated artists in the world. His large sculptures appeared in public places worldwide, one of the most famous a gigantic black stabile called *Teodelapio,* which he designed for the city of Spoleto, Italy. The piece stands over 58 feet high, and traffic drives through it. One writer called the stabile "the largest and most successful example of contemporary sculpture."

In the 1960s and 1970s Calder's posters became very popular. His style, with its bold outlines and bright colors, fit the vibrant urgency of the period perfectly. He designed numerous announcements for his own exhibitions and also contributed designs to the peace movement of the late 1960s and to environmental causes and political campaigns.

Masterworks

1926-31	*The Circus* (multimedia)
1928	*Spring* (wire sculpture)
1932	*The White Frame* (motorized sculpture)
1934	*Calderberry Bush* (mobile)
1940	*Little Spider* (mobile)
1943	*Morning Star* (stabile)
1958	*Spirale* (mobile)
1962	*Teodelapio* (stabile)
1968	*Work in Progress* (theatrical production)
1973	*Flying Colors* (DC-8 jet)
1974	*Universe* (motorized sculpture)
1975	*L'Araignée Rouge* (stabile)

Calder received a great many prizes and honors, including the Gold Medal of the American Academy of Arts and Letters in 1971 and the Grand Prix National from the French Ministry of Culture in 1974. By then his work spanned the globe. When Calder died in 1976, tributes poured in from points all over the world. Marvin Friedman, then director of the Walker Art Center in Minneapolis, eulogized the artist thus: "He was one of the greatest form-givers America has ever produced. His art was characterized by wit, invention and humanity.... His introduction of motion as a ... component of art was an unprecedented event.

Henri Cartier-Bresson

Born August 22, 1908
Chanteloup, France

"Photography is a thermometer of mood—in that way, it's like painting."

Henri Cartier-Bresson has taken a substantial portion of the twentieth century's most memorable photographs. As a photojournalist, he captured numerous crucial political developments of the 1940s and 1950s, including the Communist victory in China and the aftermath of the British Empire's departure from India. Yet he was no mere documentarian; his keen eye and sharp intelligence helped him to render scenes of universal beauty and deep emotion. Indeed, Cartier-Bresson considered himself an artist and his camera a "tool for quick drawing." He traveled the globe with his tool, and the results of these explorations have greatly influenced the way photographers, amateur and professional, see through their lenses.

The name Cartier-Bresson was as familiar in France in the early part of this century as Rockefeller or Vanderbilt were in the United States. The family fortune was made in the textile business, and Henri—the eldest of four children—remembers his father as a stern, quiet man who assumed his son would join the family enterprise like his father and grandfather. He describes his mother, on the other hand, as "extraordinarily beautiful and sensitive," a student of philosophy, psychology, and music.

Cartier-Bresson quickly lost interest in his own studies, failing to earn his baccalaureate, or high school diploma. He was, however, a great lover of poetry and philosophy and read extensively on his own; he was also an avid painter. The family spent summers at their vacation home in Normandy in the north of France, and Cartier-Bresson often visited the port of Rouen to explore the docks. He would watch the boats being loaded and frequent the sailors' taverns.

Began series of grand adventures

After secondary school Cartier-Bresson studied literature and painting for a short time at Cambridge University in England and served briefly in the army. He also studied painting in Paris with the influential teacher André Lhote. In 1931 the young man, always restless and full of energy, persuaded his grandfather to let him board an Africa-bound freighter like the ones he'd seen in Rouen, which marked the first of several grand adventures. He worked aboard the ship and then for a planter in the west African bush, and he later traveled along the coast and trekked into a coffee plantation in the interior. With his African companion, Doua, he led a primitive existence, hunting and exploring.

When Cartier-Bresson came down with a bad case of blackwater fever, or malaria, he was convinced he was dying. He sent a telegram to his grandfather saying he wanted to be buried in Normandy and have a string quartet play at his funeral. His grandfather jokingly telegraphed back that those arrangements would be too expensive and he'd do better to return home.

Cartier-Bresson did manage to return home and during his recovery he bought himself a Leica camera. It was small enough to hold in the hand—one of few available models that were so conveniently portable—and the viewfinder was attached to the body of the camera, a significant photographic innovation. It was thus remarkably light and easy to focus, the perfect instrument for an energetic young explorer. Painting and drawing, which he still loved, now seemed too slow to record "the scars of the world." Cartier-Bresson remembers that it took him three days to perfect his technique on the Leica, and he never changed his method or brand of camera. Forsaking flash, tripod, and other photographic paraphernalia, he carried his camera in his hand, taking his shots quickly and quietly and never shooting too many photos of the same scene.

Master of capturing the "decisive moment"

It was a simple technique, but it succeeded thanks to Cartier-Bresson's natural ability to position himself at a scene and press the shutter button at just the instant when the background, lighting, and composition of the scene were exactly right. Few photographers have achieved a comparable degree of skill even after years of experimentation. Cartier-Bresson reportedly was fond of saying that he couldn't take a photograph—the photograph took him. He had an uncanny capacity for predicting "the decisive moment" of an event and framing it through the camera. This phrase "decisive moment," in fact, became something of a motto for his work and was the English title of a book of his photographs published in 1952.

Once he found his camera, the rest of Cartier-Bresson's life—as the saying goes—was history. And much of what he shot was indeed historically monumental. On several continents, through political upheavals and quiet moments alike, he let the photographs take him. In the 1930s he traveled in Africa, Spain, Italy, and Mexico. It was in Mexico, after he was stranded there when a job fell through, that he began what would eventually become his standard practice: roaming the streets and mixing with the inhabitants thereof. He thus found photographic subjects wherever he went.

By 1934 Cartier-Bresson's photographs had been exhibited in Madrid, Mexico City, and New York. These shows included photos he had taken in Spain of unemployed workers, children playing in ruined buildings, and, one of his most famous, the *Callejon of the Valencia Arena*. This photo depicts a uniformed man looking through a wooden gate at a bullfight arena. One eyepiece of his glasses has caught the sunlight at

such an angle that it looks as though he has a hole in his head. At the show in New York, his works were called "antigraphic photographs" because it was thought they were unplanned and accidental. Amateur photography had become more popular as the availability of small cameras became widespread. Cartier-Bresson's name became associated with the mania for snapshots, and in his quest for the "decisive moment" he had many imitators.

Family of Newsvendors, Mexico City, *1934.*
Reproduced by permission of Magnum Photos, Inc.

Captured by Nazis

In 1935 Cartier-Bresson left photography for a time to study filmmaking. He served as second assistant to the great French director Jean Renoir, working on scripts and scouting locations. At the outbreak of World War II in 1939, he was drafted into the

Banks of the Marne, 1938. Gelatin silver print photograph, 23.3 cm x 34.8 cm. The Museum of Modern Art, New York. © Henri Cartier-Bresson/ Magnum Photos, Inc.

French army; in June of the following year, his unit was captured by the Nazis and he spent three years in forced labor in Germany. He was caught twice attempting to escape, but on his third try he made it back to Paris, where he joined the underground resistance against the Germans as a photojournalist. At the end of the war he made a film for the U.S. Office of War Information about prisoners of war returning to France. He had planned to go back to painting, he told an interviewer for the *New York Times* in 1994. "It proved impossible," he said. "Photography seemed right for seeing what was happening in the world."

In 1947 Cartier-Bresson and several other photographers founded the Magnum Photo Agency, which enabled them to work as independent photographers and sell their pictures to newspapers and magazines. For Magnum, Cartier-Bresson undertook assignments around the world. First he went to Asia, capturing large-scale developments as well as the fine points of everyday life. He spent a long time in India, covering its early years of independence from the British. He then went to China and recorded the political chaos leading up to—and including—the

Communist victory. He was also in Indonesia in the first months after that country gained independence from the Dutch. In later years Cartier-Bresson recalled the excitement of those times, remarking, "It is a tremendous joy to be there, the physical feeling of being on the crest of a wave with a camera the size of your hand." With his keen eye, his feeling for people and place, and his interest in local traditions, he was able to express the beauty in even the most seemingly mundane landscape and communicate the humanity of all peoples. Much of Cartier-Bresson's work appeared in exhibitions in the 1950s and 1960s, as well as in magazines and several books.

In 1970 Cartier-Bresson married a photographer, Martine Franck. They have lived in Paris ever since, as has their daughter. Over the years he returned to drawing. "I've never been interested in photography per se," he told the *New York Times*. "For me, photography is instant drawing. My real obsession is drawing." Even at the age of 85 he spent many hours sketching in his studio or at the Louvre museum.

Cartier-Bresson's brilliant reputation, nonetheless, derives from his photography. To celebrate his eightieth birthday in 1988, a large exhibition was mounted in Paris; it traveled to New York in 1994 to celebrate his eighty-sixth birthday. The show included 40 of his most famous photos and the premiere of a film about his work. Unfortunately, heart surgery prevented him from attending the celebration. Still, Cartier-Bresson's energy and intelligence have not waned. He continues to carry his camera with him and shoots occasional photographs, "mostly portraits of friends and people I meet.... For me, the passion is to look, to look, to look."

Masterworks

1932	*Behind Gare St. Lazar*
1933	*Children Playing in Ruins, Spain*
	Callejon of the Valencia Arena
1938	*Banks of the Marne*
	Hyde Park, London
1944	*Henri Matisse, Vence*
1948	*Shanghai, When Gold Was on Sale During the Last Days of the Kuomintang*
1953	*Abruzzi, Italy*
1961	*Alberto Giacometti*

Mary Cassatt

Born May 22, 1844
Allegheny, Pennsylvania
Died June 14, 1926
Mesnil-Théribus, France

"After all, give me France. Women do not have to fight for recognition here if they do serious work."

Mary Cassatt had at least two strikes against her as an aspiring artist in Paris in the 1870s and 1880s: she was an American, and she was a woman. Her strong will, intellect, and talent, however, proved sufficient to meet this challenge and earned her the respect of her colleagues, especially Edgar Degas, as well as the admiration of art critics and the general public. She studied and respected the work of past masters but blazed her own trail, influenced significantly by **impressionism** and Japanese art. Of her various works, her gentle, expressive, and vividly real portraits of mothers and children have received the most acclaim. Through her social contacts with wealthy collectors of the time, she also shouldered the responsibility of bringing numerous works of French impressionism to the United States.

Mary Stevenson Cassatt enjoyed a comfortable, upper-middle-class upbringing. She was the fifth child of Katherine Kelso Johnston and Robert Simpson Cassatt, the latter a successful real estate and banking investor. The family moved often during Mary's childhood, from the Pittsburgh area, where she was born, to Philadelphia when she was about five and then to Europe two years later. Like most girls of the time, she was expected to grow up to become a wife and mother, so her education included household management, embroidery, art, and music.

Culturally rich childhood in Paris

The Cassatts settled in Paris in 1851 and remained there for several years. They made sure that their children experienced the myriad cultural advantages of that most cosmopolitan of cities, providing them with French lessons and arranging outings to art museums; living in such a culturally charged environment made a tremendous impression on Mary. The family moved to Germany in 1855 but stayed only a few months, returning to Philadelphia after the sudden death of Mary's 13-year-old brother, Robbie.

Philadelphia was then the second-largest city in the United States and as such boasted an active cultural and artistic community, which included the Pennsylvania Academy of the Fine Arts, a museum and art school. Cassatt enrolled at the Academy when she was 16, having decided that she wanted to become a professional artist. Her family did not encourage her in this pursuit; it was considered unseemly for women—especially those from socially prominent and prosperous families—to have careers.

The Pennsylvania Academy had earned a reputation as a progressive institution because it was one of the few art schools in the country that admitted women. Nonetheless, the curriculum was not especially progressive; it consisted largely of copying traditional paintings and sculptures and drawing realistic, or highly representational, views of live models. After two years Cassatt was frustrated by both the conservative approach to teaching and the attitude of the male teachers and students toward women students. Since liberal admission policies did not guarantee a dynamic environment, she gravitated toward the most forward-looking cultural climate she had thus far experienced. The best way to learn about art, she became convinced, would be to go to Europe and study it on her own. In 1866 she returned to Paris.

During the next two years Cassatt took private art lessons and copied masterpieces at the Louvre, France's national art museum, lavishing particular attention on the art of sixteenth-century Italian painter Correggio, German painter Holbein, and seventeenth-century Spanish court painter **Diego Velazquez** (see entry). She traveled around France, painting in the countryside, and briefly visited Rome. And she was able to observe some of the new developments in French painting, including works by Edgar Degas and **Claude Monet** (see entry), at the Paris **Salon** exhibition of 1866. The government's Academy of Fine Arts sponsored the Salon exhibits, participation in which had by this time become a prerequisite for a successful career as an artist. But in the 1860s a group of young artists began to rebel against the conservative, traditional offerings sponsored by the Academy. They shocked the art world by daring to paint scenes from modern life and challenging the dominance of classical notions of beauty and symmetry. This group became the core of the school of impressionism and included Degas and Monet, as well as **Pierre-Auguste Renoir** and **Edouard Manet** (see entries), Camille Pissarro, and others. When some of Cassatt's paintings were accepted into the Salons of 1868 and 1870, she was pleased but at the same time felt stifled by the styles approved by the judges. She was increasingly drawn to the vivid colors and innovative philosophy and technique of the impressionists.

Paintings lost in Chicago fire of 1871

In 1870 Cassatt returned to the States to escape the war then raging between France and Prussia. She lived with her parents in a small town outside Philadelphia and planned to return to Europe as soon as the situation permitted. Because few people were willing to model for her and art supplies were hard to find, she found it almost impossible to paint in this provincial American locale. To compound an already difficult circumstance, her father refused to pay for any expenses incurred by her art work. In 1871 she took some of her paintings to a dealer in Chicago; tragically, most of them were destroyed in the great fire there that year.

Cassatt's discouragement grew until, finally, she received a commission from a bishop in Philadelphia to travel to Italy and copy two religious paintings by Correggio in a church in Parma. She lived in the town for several months and, in the course of copying the paintings, had her first experience painting babies, which was to become her trademark in later years. During these months she also worked on her own paintings and finished enough to submit to exhibitions in France and the United States.

Cassatt used the money she earned from this commission to settle back in Paris and begin painting. One of her paintings was accepted into the Salon in 1872 and another two years later. Yet she still experienced doubt about her success in the vein favored by the **academic art** establishment, preferring her own style, with its livelier colors, freer brush strokes, and modern subjects. She was also encouraged by seeing some paintings by Degas in a gallery window and knowing there were other artists with similar ideas. In fact, Degas had seen her painting at the 1874 Salon and had been impressed. It was at this time that he and his fellow artists were planning an independent exhibit to demonstrate their rejection of the academic style, at which their method was first labeled impressionism.

Befriends Degas, formally joins impressionists

Cassatt and Degas were introduced by a mutual friend in 1877. They had admired each other's work for several years and found that they liked each other immensely and shared a variety of ideas. Degas invited Cassatt to display her paintings with the impressionists in their 1879 exhibit. She never again submitted work to a juried show such as the Salon. Joining the impressionists seemed to free her from the expectations of the Salon and allow her to paint without reservation in her own style.

Cassatt's friendship with Degas grew, and though their strong personalities sometimes clashed, they inspired one another creatively. Sometimes they painted the same scene, and his renderings of people in the theaters and dance halls of Paris

Mary Cassatt

had a marked influence on her work. Her 1882 painting *The Loge,* a scene of two women in a box at the theater, reveals Cassatt's change to pastel colors and unrestrained rendering of objects like flowers. Cassatt and Degas also worked together on **engraving,** etching in metal plates to make prints of their drawings. Cassatt devoted many years to the precise art of printmaking.

Cassatt's style differed from those of a number of her fellow impressionists because she generally favored portraiture over landscapes or city scenes. Paintings of women at home, often with their children, became a recurrent theme. Her work usually elicited favorable reviews and as an American and a woman, she often found herself in the limelight. Becoming acquainted with other women artists of the time such as Berthe Morisot and Eva Gonzales affected her life dramatically; these women were among the few accepted professionally by the male-dominated art world.

At the height of her career—the 1870s and 1880s—Cassatt was forced to stop painting on several occasions in order to care for family members who were ill. Her parents and sister had joined her in Paris in 1877, and her sister became ill shortly thereafter and died in 1882; Cassatt's mother was ill during this time as well. Mary tended to their needs and ran the household, which left her very little time for painting. At times she also had to leave Paris to accompany her mother to warmer climates, excursions designed to improve her failing health. Cassatt's determination to paint never faltered, however, and her style evolved constantly as she experimented with new approaches to color, space, and composition. Her 1886 painting *Girl Arranging Her Hair* displays more controlled brushwork and the artist's movement away from the looser impressionist tendency. She painted this scene of a rather homely young woman to prove to Degas that a beautiful painting does not depend on the beauty of the model, just the skill of the artist.

◀ Mother and Infant. *Pastel. Reproduced by permission of Giraudon/Art Resource, NY.*

Encouraged sale of impressionist works in America

Cassatt strongly encouraged her family and friends from the States to buy the paintings of the impressionists; her brother Alexander eventually owned 20 pieces. She was a deciding factor in her friend Louisine Elder Havemeyer's becoming one of the earliest collectors of impressionist art in the United States. The Havemeyer collection was eventually donated to the Metropolitan Museum of Art in New York City and can still be seen there.

Cassatt's busy schedule reached a peak of activity in the 1890s. In addition to dispensing advice to the throng of young American artists who sought her out, she began working on what would become her signature paintings of mothers and children, for which she used her nieces and nephews as models. A major change in Cassatt's style came when she and Degas attended an exhibition of Japanese art in 1890. She immediately incorporated the bold lines and flat areas of color and pattern she saw there into her work. *Feeding the Ducks, The Letter,* and *The Boating Party* all provide evidence of the concepts Cassatt began exploring in the early 1890s. Her ability to experiment with and adapt new ideas kept her style fresh.

Cassatt's success brought financial independence, and she was eventually able to purchase a house in a small town near Paris; she divided her time there between painting in her spacious studio and tending the garden. In 1893 she was commissioned to paint a **mural** for the World's Columbian Exhibition in Chicago. Cassatt's work had not achieved much visibility in the United States, and she hoped to use this opportunity to make a name for herself there. Unfortunately the massive project turned out to involve more difficulty than Cassatt had anticipated and because she was not in Chicago to see the building for which the mural was intended, her efforts were ultimately incompatible with the style of the building and the other artworks housed there. The experience was a major disappointment. Later that year, how-

◀ Sara in a Green Bonnet, *1901. Oil on canvas, 16⅝" x 13⅝". National Museum of American Art, Washington, DC/Art Resource, NY.*

Masterworks

1878	*Reading Le Figaro*
	Little Girl in a Blue Armchair
1880	*Five O'clock Tea*
1882	*The Loge*
1884-85	*Alexander Cassatt and His Son Robert*
1886	*Girl Arranging Her Hair*
1890-91	*The Letter*
1891-92	*The Bath*
1893-94	*The Boating Party*
1894	*Feeding the Ducks*
1897	*Breakfast in Bed*
1901	*Child with Red Hat*

ever, Cassatt had her first solo exhibition in New York, which was a success. One reviewer wrote, "No painter has seen so much feeling, nor has anyone, with such convincing art, translated into canvas the poem of the family." Cassatt was soon considered one of the most important American artists residing in Europe.

In 1895 Cassatt was devastated by the death of her mother, the last family member for whom she had been caring. She was alone for the first time in her life, and her work seemed to suffer for it. She spent increasing time advising American collectors who came to Paris to buy artworks and embarked on various travels, including a trip to Egypt with her brother and his family in 1910. This journey had a negative impact overall, for Cassatt was apparently overwhelmed by the beauty of the country and its ancient art and lost confidence in her own skills. Even more distressing, her brother became ill during the excursion and died suddenly after their return. Shortly after this Cassatt found her eyesight growing dim from diabetes; consequently, she was unable to spend much time painting.

Cassatt lived to be 82 years old, long enough to enjoy the lofty heights of fame and respect she'd won in the art world. She was very modest about her work, believing that women shouldn't engage in self-promotion. She also refused many laurels that were offered her, having pledged that after joining the impressionist "rebels" she would not submit her work to judges or accept honors. One award she did accept, however, was the Legion of Honor, presented to her by the French government in 1904. It was unusual for this medal to be bestowed on a woman—doubly so to an American. Two years after her death, four exhibitions of Cassatt's work were mounted in the United States, the largest in her hometown of Philadelphia. Finally, her accomplishments had been recognized at home, her talent and determination ever a testament to the creative spirit.

Paul Cézanne

Born January 19, 1839
Aix-en-Provence, France
Died October 22, 1906
Aix-en-Provence, France

Lonely, cantankerous, and ridiculed as a madman, Paul Cézanne was nonetheless one of the most important paint ers of his century. Combining traditional forms with a modern expressiveness, Cézanne's art received little recognition until late in his life, but it has exercised a profound influence on painters throughout the twentieth century. More than 40 years after Cézanne's death, three esteemed painters declared, "We are all descended from Cézanne."

The course of much of Cézanne's life was determined by the actions and opinions of his strong, domineering father, Louis-Auguste Cézanne. An ambitious man who made a fortune in the hat-making industry, the senior Cézanne became the most successful banker in the family's hometown. He married an employee of one of his hat shops, Anne-Elisabeth-Honorine Aubert, and fathered three children—Paul and his two younger sisters. The family enjoyed a comfortable life in the beautiful town of Aix in the south of France, eventually inhabiting a large estate outside the village. This region provided Cézanne with the exquisite scenery that he painted throughout his career.

"There is a passing moment in the world. Paint it in all its reality. Forget everything else for that."

▲ *Portrait:* Self-portrait, *c. 1877-80. Reproduced by permission of Giraudon/ Art Resource, NY.*

Social development hampered by domineering father

Socially awkward and emotionally sensitive, Cézanne suffered from bouts of depression and harbored a violent streak that caused him to fly into sudden rages. His often unfounded distrust discouraged enduring friendships. Scholars trace many of Cézanne's problems to his family life and particularly his father, who thought him incompetent and treated him like a child well into the artist's adulthood. Cézanne feared his father, yet he relied on him for his financial needs throughout his life. This dependence caused considerable resentment. Cézanne was similarly constrained in social relationships by his reliance on his mother and one of his sisters for emotional support. He spent much of his time alone.

One crucial lasting relationship, however, was with his boyhood friend Émile Zola; the two were inseparable during their school years and remained close for much of their lives. It was Zola who eventually convinced Cézanne to join him in Paris and make a serious attempt at a career in art, and his correspondence with the artist has provided much of what historians know about him. Zola supported and encouraged Cézanne during many years of frustration, introducing the painter to a variety of Parisian artists. But in 1886, Zola—one of the most popular and controversial writers in France—wrote a novel the main character of which, a failed painter, was obviously modeled on Cézanne. This portrayal effectively ended the friendship, though Cézanne was deeply saddened by Zola's death in 1902.

Cézanne's education emphasized the humanities and religious instruction. He was a good student and received awards in math, Latin, and Greek, but he showed little prowess in his art classes. After he graduated from secondary school, his father insisted that he study law, which he did unwillingly for two years. During this time he decided to try painting as a career, establishing a studio at home. At Zola's urging he finally went to Paris for a few months in 1861, a period that proved both exciting and frustrating. Despite the pleasure he took in viewing the masterpieces of the Louvre museum—not to mention the often impressive work of his contemporaries—his lack of training and

technical skill vexed him. His increasing depression drove him back to Aix, where he worked in his father's bank for a year.

Discovered emotional release in painting

Again it was his friend Zola who encouraged him to return to Paris. By this time Cézanne sought to vent his emotional distress through his painting. His work from this early period displays a preoccupation with violence and fantasy; it was roundly scorned as wild and undisciplined. This caused Cézanne more anxiety, but he continued in the endeavor because he had found in painting a medium for portraying his tumultuous inner state.

Even so, Cézanne did not spend these years in complete solitude. Indeed, he had some contact with a group of young Parisian artists working to challenge the art world's traditions.

Card Players, 1892. 18½" x 22½". Musée d'Orsay, Paris. Reproduced by permission of Giraudon/ Art Resource, NY.

These included **Claude Monet, Pierre-Auguste Renoir,** and **Edouard Manet** (see entries). Camille Pissarro also befriended Cézanne, painting with him and perhaps serving as a sympathetic father figure. All of these artists strove to define a new artistic vision against what they regarded as the staid classicism maintained by traditionalists. They shocked the art world by painting their "impressions" of scenes from everyday life. Their attempts to render the nuances of their environment became known as **impressionism.** Cézanne experimented with numerous impressionist concepts—especially those regarding color and the attempt to capture a certain moment in time—but the style he eventually developed was more structured and intense than that of the impressionists.

It took Cézanne many years to refine his style; well into the late 1860s he sought a more disciplined means to render his inner landscape on canvas. One of the first paintings to show this new control is a **still life,** *The Black Clock.* It provides the earliest glimpses of Cézanne's use of broad areas of color and his deployment of horizontal and vertical lines for structure. He gave this painting to his friend Zola.

Around the same time, Cézanne began a relationship with a young woman named Marie-Hortense Figuet. Though little is known about her, it is certain that she figured prominently in the painter's life; over the years, Cézanne painted more than 40 portraits of her. They married in 1886, 14 years after the birth of their son, Paul. His general social difficulty notwithstanding, Cézanne maintained a loving relationship with his son, occasionally using him as a model and letting the boy draw in his sketch books. He spent as much time with him as possible, though Madame Cézanne and the younger Paul lived mostly in Paris, while Cézanne spent his time painting in Aix. Troubled family relationships were partly responsible for the separation. Cézanne, meanwhile, never told his father about his relationship with Marie-Hortense or about the existence of their son. When the elder Cézanne died in 1886, he left the painter enough money to ensure his financial security for the rest of his life; Cézanne no longer had to struggle to earn a living from his art. This stability may have contributed to a greater freedom to experiment in his work.

The 1870s saw Cézanne continuing the gradual refinement of his style. He lived for a time in L'Estaque, a small town on the Mediterranean Sea, in order to avoid serving in the army during France's war with Prussia. The area figured prominently in his landscape paintings thenceforth; these views of L'Estaque and of a mountain near Aix called Mont Sainte-Victoire are among Cézanne's most celebrated landscapes.

Called a madman

At last, in the 1870s, Cézanne's work began to attract attention from critics and patrons. While a few patrons saw potential in his work, most critics disapproved—some going so far as to call him a "madman." These negative reviews, which continued throughout his life, did not stop Cézanne from painting, but they did deepen his despondence and withdrawal from others. Viewers had difficulty understanding that Cézanne was interested in revealing more than just "the scene itself," that he sought instead to render his subjects through the prism of his own experience. He frequently employed geometric shapes to create form, and he declared that artists should "see in nature the cylinder, the sphere, and the cone." Color, rather than traditional **perspective,** define space in his work.

These techniques were quite shocking to Cézanne's traditionally oriented contemporaries. Rather than provide the comforting illusion of looking through a window, as if the canvas and paint did not exist, Cézanne chose to emphasize the emotions of the artist and the viewer over the precise depiction of the subject painted. It was only a short step to the centrality of the artwork—that is, the work's focus on itself, a fundamental component of twentieth-century artistic thought. Cézanne's forays into these untried waters were vitally important to the development of such twentieth-century styles as **cubism, fauvism, abstract expressionism,** and **surrealism.** Many consider his work a crucial link between the movements of impressionism and cubism.

These radical ideas came into focus for Cézanne in the 1880s and 1890s, when he worked completely alone. Most of what we know about his life during this period comes from his letters to Zola. He moved his residence constantly between Paris and Aix, seemingly even less able to interact with society as he gained artistic confidence. In fact, he was such a recluse that a number of people believed he had died. Others wondered about the old man who tramped around the mountains in his boots and floppy hat, carrying an easel and paintbox. In addition to landscapes, Cézanne painted numerous still lifes of objects from his home and studio—pieces of fruit, wine bottles, vases, dishes. Cézanne no doubt preferred still lifes because they did not involve uncomfortable human contact with a model and permitted him to work slowly and carefully. Sometimes he spent months on one scene.

Mounted first solo show at age 56

He also painted portraits, many of himself and of Mme. Cézanne. But he found it frustrating to paint other people, insisting that they sit frozen for hours on end and becoming angry if they moved. He snapped to one restless model, "You must sit like an apple. Does an apple move?" Cézanne painted more than 300 canvases during this time; in the words of one art historian, "Among them are most of the paintings from his brush that affected the early course of 20th Century art." Painters like **Henri Matisse, Pablo Picasso,** and **Paul Gauguin** (see entries) drew inspiration from his work. But it was not until 1895, when Cézanne was 56 years old, that he had his first solo show. His reputation among artists was growing and the show was fairly well received. But many traditionalists still considered his work wild and outrageous.

Masterworks

1869	*The Black Clock*
1877	*Madame Cézanne in a Red Armchair*
1879	*Self-Portrait*
1883	*L'Estaque*
1888	*Still Life with Fruit Basket*
1892	*The Bathers*
1898	*Mont Sainte-Victoire from Bibémus Quarry*
1906	*River at the Bridge of the Three Springs*

During the last decades of his life, as young artists and critics began to seek out this controversial painter, Cézanne grew increasingly moody, suspicious, and absorbed by his work. Still, his paintings from these years are among his most free-flowing, colorful, and spontaneous. Despite declining health, Cézanne worked every day, using watercolors when oil paints became too difficult to handle. During the last summer of his life, he painted along the banks of a river by his home, near where he and Zola had swum in their youth. These paintings, among them *River at the Bridge of the Three Springs,* seem surprisingly contemporary, though they were produced in 1906. The extreme heat of that summer and a case of pneumonia weakened Cézanne; he died the following fall.

True recognition of Cézanne's genius began almost immediately after his death. Even the town of Aix, which had ignored him and his creations, eventually came to honor the artist with a bronze medallion, designed by Pierre-Auguste Renoir, which was mounted on a fountain in the town square. Several twentieth-century art movements claim Cézanne as their father, one art historian noting that "his work clarified the vision and aim of painting."

Marc Chagall

*Born July 7, 1887
Pestkowatik (Vitebsk), Russia
Died March 28, 1985
Saint-Paul-de-Vence, France*

"I don't understand my paintings at all. They are only pictorial arrangements of images that obsess me. My paintings are my reason for existence, my life and that's all."

The painting style of Marc Chagall ranks among the most readily identifiable of the twentieth century. His work provides the preeminent example of modern visual art featuring Jewish themes, which incorporates folklore and dreamscapes into a deeply personal and mystical painterly language. Although he lived in France for much of his adult life, a substantial number of his works are based on scenes of the Russian village of his childhood. Chagall was a man possessed of enormous energy and love of life. Though his fame derives primarily from his painting, he also worked in prints and etchings, book illustrations, stained glass, sculpture, and ceramics, and designed sets and costumes for the theater and ballet.

Circumstances weighed against the odds of Chagall—the son of Zahar and Feiga-Ita Chagall—becoming an artist; as devout Jews his parents adhered strictly to the biblical commandment against the making of "graven images." There were no artworks on the walls of their small home, which was situated in a village in the Pale of Settlement, near the Russian-Polish border,

Marc Chagall | 64

the only area in Russia where Jews were permitted to live. Like the other villages in the area, it was dreary and its inhabitants mostly poor. Chagall's father worked in the warehouse of a herring dealer, while his mother managed a small grocery store and raised the couple's eight children.

Declines career as herring hauler

Chagall began attending a traditional religious school at about six years of age. Of special interest to him were Bible stories, which contained characters that seemed as real to him as the peasants, merchants, and rabbis of his village. When he was ten the family moved to the nearby town of Vitebsk, the capital of the province. Chagall went to public school there but was not a good student; he enjoyed only geometry and drawing. As his teenage years progressed, he began to contemplate his future. He knew he did not want to haul barrels of fish, as his father did, or follow in the footsteps of his uncles, who were butchers and rabbis. The direction that most attracted him was art. He spent much of his free time drawing, recording the buildings and people around him, and dreaming of escaping the idleness of village life.

Chagall convinced his parents to let him enroll in a local art school, but his excitement quickly dulled; the curriculum involved copying classical sculptures and various "realistic" drawings and paintings. The time he spent there was not completely wasted, though, since he acquired such skills as mixing paints and preparing a canvas and clean brushes. He also met other young people who shared his passion for art.

While at school Chagall had been doing retouching work (removing imperfections) for a local photographer. This occupation was unstimulating, but it earned him a small income. When one of his schoolmates asked Chagall to move with him to the capital city, St. Petersburg, to study art, he eagerly agreed. Yet several obstacles remained. Chief among them was that neither he nor his family had the necessary funds. Also, he needed government clearance to be in the city. Under the rule of the czars, the emperors who controlled Russia, Jews experienced severe repression; they were considered foreigners even if their families

Portrait (p. 64): **Self-portrait with Seven Fingers,** *1912-13. Amsterdam Stedelijk Museum. © 1995 Artists Rights Society (ARS), New York/ADAGP, Paris. Foto Marburg/Art Resource, NY.*

had lived in Russia for many generations, and they were not allowed to live in the cities or even hold certain jobs without special permits, which were difficult to secure. Chagall's father was, nonetheless, able to obtain a temporary permit for the artist to reside in St. Petersburg, and he traveled there when he was 19 years old.

Suffers in St. Petersburg

Chagall lived in the city intermittently for roughly three years and endured a range of hardships, including jail time for possession of an expired permit, as well as suffering cold and hunger. He tried several schools but found them too traditional and conservative; finally, he found the Svantseva School, run by Leon Bakst, an artist who had studied in Paris and was familiar with many of the most cutting-edge, or **avant-garde,** styles of art in Europe. Chagall's work advanced quite a bit at this school, in part because he had his first exposure (through printed copies) to the work of French **impressionist Paul Cézanne,** Dutch **expressionist Vincent van Gogh,** French post-impressionist **Paul Gauguin,** and French **fauvist Henri Matisse** (see entries). They were among the most popular artists of the time in Europe. Chagall was influenced by some aspects of these artists' work, but his own style was developing apace. His teacher, Bakst, wrote of Chagall that "after listening closely to my lessons, he takes his paints and brushes and does something absolutely different."

Chagall's paintings from this period, when he was in his early twenties, depict scenes from his village, such as weddings and festivals. Even with such happy subjects, his intentional use of muted color helped convey the oppression and difficulty of life in the provinces of Russia. He also painted the first of many portraits of Bella Rosenfeld, who would become his wife. *Portrait of My Fiancée with Black Gloves* is a romantic view of this young woman that also reveals her strength and intelligence. Bella was Chagall's chief support and companion for roughly 30 years. Before they were

◄ I and the Village, *1911. Oil on canvas, 6'3⅝" x 4' 11⅝". The Museum of Modern Art, New York. Mrs. Simon Guggenheim Fund. Photograph © 1995 The Museum of Modern Art, New York.*

married, however, Chagall took a major step toward advancing his career: he left Russia in 1910 and went to live in Paris. It was a wrenching decision to leave his family and Bella behind, but he was fortunate enough to find a patron who believed in his future as an artist and who paid him an allowance for his living expenses.

The Paris that Chagall discovered at the age of 23 was the center of European culture. Artists, writers, scholars, and musicians gathered there to experience the air of electric creativity. Chagall was swept up by this environment and felt he had found his spiritual home. Among the first things he did in Paris was visit the Louvre, the enormous national art museum, which contains paintings by the great masters. He also visited galleries to see the work of artists like Cézanne, Matisse, and Spanish cubist **Pablo Picasso** (see entry).

A poet who used paint instead of words

Chagall spent about four years in Paris. This was among the most creative periods of his life and facilitated the fuller development of his deeply personal style. His paintings, often recalling his life in Russia or aspects of his Jewish heritage, were luminously colorful and often influenced by the innovations of the cubists, who were very active in Paris at the time. Chagall was not a supporter of **cubism**, but he used its method of breaking up the parts of a subject or scene to give his paintings their dreamlike quality: animals and people float in the air, depictions of objects are not limited by realistic proportions, and color seems to be applied at random. One of his most celebrated works from this time is *I and the Village*. Other artists of the era considered Chagall a poet who used paint instead of words. As poets alter words, spelling, and punctuation to communicate their feelings, Chagall changed space, color, and shapes as he felt necessary. He had less interest than had the cubists in formal experimentation for its own sake; his primary concern was depicting his inner life. He found admiration and respect among the prominent writers and artists of the day, but the public often had difficulty understanding his mystical, multicolored fantasies.

Because of this lack of public acceptance, in addition to his lack of affiliation with any established school of painting, Chagall found it difficult to secure exhibition space and thus sell his paintings. Finally, in 1914, a poet friend introduced Chagall to a German writer and art dealer who set up the artist's first solo exhibit, which took place in Berlin rather than Paris. The exhibition was a success and helped inaugurate widespread recognition for Chagall's work. He went from Berlin to visit his family in Vitebsk, and while he was there, in August 1914, World War I broke out. As travel was impossible during the war, the artist was trapped in Russia.

Although Chagall found he had outgrown his hometown after his many experiences in Paris, he used the time there to paint; he created almost 60 works in one year. He and Bella were married in July 1915 and moved to St. Petersburg, where Chagall landed a desk job at the Russian Department of War Economy in order to avoid being drafted into the service. The job was dull, but it afforded him ample opportunity to paint, and he saw the growth of his reputation as one of the finest painters in Russia. He painted some scenes of country life as he spent time outside the city and after his daughter's birth in 1916, he painted portraits of her. Soldiers also became his subjects, for his depictions of war's agonies.

When World War I ended in 1917, an even more significant event confronted Chagall: the Russian Revolution. This political and social upheaval changed the country forever and led eventually to the formation of the communist government. The early years of the revolution were exciting and dangerous, and Chagall felt he should stay and participate in his nation's rebirth rather than return to Paris as he had planned. Because of his great reputation, he was appointed minister of culture for Vitebsk and was given the job of turning his village into a center for the arts, with museums and an art school. He worked with great energy and in 1919 opened the Free Academy of the Arts. Unfortunately, within a year, the internal politics of the school became so complicated that Chagall resigned in anger and went to live in Moscow.

Paints State Jewish Theater murals

Life in this principal Russian city was very difficult, but Chagall was able to work in the theater there. Because Jews by that point had gained a measure of political and religious freedom, a revival of Jewish culture blossomed. An acquaintance of Chagall's was founding the State Jewish Theater and asked the artist to design sets and costumes and to paint **murals** for the theater's new auditorium. Chagall's enthusiasm led him to take over all aspects of the production. The murals he painted, titled *Introduction to the Jewish Theater,* were joyous and lively, featuring clowns, musicians, acrobats, and actors. Although Chagall loved his work, he was not compensated for it, and he found it more and more difficult to support his family. He began to feel that he would be unable to forge a career as an artist in Russia.

In 1922 he received a letter from a friend in Berlin reporting that rumors of his death had made him famous and that his paintings were commanding high prices. This clinched his decision to return to Paris and after a stop of several months in Berlin, Chagall, Bella, and their daughter arrived in Paris in September 1923. For the next 18 years, until World War II forced him to leave France, Chagall experienced a period of great creativity and success. He was commissioned to do illustrations, **etchings** on metal plates that could be printed, for several books, including the classic Russian novel *Dead Souls* by Nikolai Gogol, La Fontaine's French translation of *Aesop's Fables,* and the Bible, the illustrations for which he began after a trip to the Middle East in 1931. Chagall's extensive travels during the 1930s included visits to Holland, where he studied the works of portrait master **Rembrandt van Rijn** (see entry), to Spain, where he was influenced by the paintings of seventeenth-century court painter **Diego Velazquez** and his nineteenth-century successor **Francisco Goya** (see entries), and to Italy to study the masters Donatello and **Titian** (see entry).

Chagall's paintings of the 1920s and 1930s demonstrate numerous transformations in style and content, though the essential characteristics of his sensibility remained. His travels and vacations around France inspired him to paint more scenes of nature and particularly motivated the inclusion of flowers in a substantial number of his paintings. There were colorful, light-hearted paintings of circus performers, lovers in trees, angels, and animals. He did not leave behind his memories of Russia, however, and many works portray his dreamlike memories. *The Green Violinist,* one of his most famous paintings, depicts a musician (possibly one of Chagall's uncles) with a green face and hands dancing on the village rooftops. Yet he also addressed the more sober themes of Russian life and of Jewish culture during the 1930s and was greatly concerned with political events in Europe, especially the rise of Adolf Hitler and the Nazi party in Germany; many of his works from this time have a sense of tragedy and menace about them.

Flees Nazi terrorism

Chagall did not want to leave Nazi-occupied France during World War II, but as the government began passing severely anti-Jewish laws and sending Jews to concentration camps, he realized that he had no choice. In May 1941, the Chagall family crossed the border into Spain and then into Portugal, where they boarded a cargo ship and endured a 43-day journey to New York. Artists and dealers who knew and admired Chagall's work helped him get settled, and his daughter had managed to pack up and send to New York all of his paintings and drawings, so he was able to continue working. He worked again in the theater, where he designed sets and costumes for several ballets, including one that premiered in Mexico.

Tragedy struck in September 1944 when Bella Chagall developed a viral infection and died suddenly. She had been such an important inspiration to Chagall for more than three decades that he was unable to work for nine months. "Everything went dark before my eyes," he wrote. He began to recover in 1945 when he was afforded a chance to work on the ballet *The Firebird* by the Russian composer Igor Stravinsky.

In 1946 and 1947, with the war over, Chagall was able to visit Paris again, and he settled in France permanently in 1948. By this time he was considered one of the most important art-

ists in the world. He continued to work with great energy, tackling larger canvases and employing even more dazzling colors. He participated in several ballet and opera productions in the 1950s and 1960s and also began to work in ceramics and in clay and stone sculpture. At 70 he learned the intricate art of stained glass; for almost 20 years he designed magnificent windows for synagogues, churches, and other buildings in

Europe, the United States, and Israel. In 1973 he established a museum near his home in the south of France to house the works he'd completed over some 30 years that depicted Biblical subjects. That year he also returned to Russia (then the Soviet Union) for the first time in almost 50 years. It was a powerfully emotional experience for the painter to revisit the source of so much of his inspiration.

Chagall continued working vigorously until his death in 1985 at the age of 97. His work was truly revolutionary in its expansion of the boundaries of art to include dreams, fantasy, and emotional—rather than geographical—landscapes. He was able to use his remarkable life experiences and Russian-Jewish heritage as inspiration and source material, though the appeal of his work respects no cultural borders. One admirer deemed Chagall a "magician who gave wings not only to animals, but to the imagination of [people] as well."

Masterworks

1909	*Russian Wedding*
	Portrait of My Fiancée with Black Gloves
1911	*I and the Village*
1912	*Self-Portrait with Seven Fingers*
1913	*Paris through the Window*
1915	*Birthday*
1917	*Double Portrait with Wine Glass*
1923	*Green Violinist*
1930-39	*Time Is a River without Banks*
1964-66	*War*

Judy Chicago

Born July 20, 1939
Chicago, Illinois

"I have always believed that art is important—in fact central—to human life. This act is what has always sustained me, no matter how difficult my life has sometimes been."

Judy Chicago is one of the foremost feminist artists in the United States. A painter, sculptor, writer, educator, and performer, she has also worked in ceramics, plastics, needlework, and china painting. Chicago's long personal struggle to find her role as a woman artist has produced some of the most controversial and fascinating works of recent decades, many of them addressing the place of women in history and society. Moreover, Chicago has been a leader in the movement to discover important women artists of the past and to educate young women to be active creators of the future.

She was born Judy Gerowitz to a middle-class family in Chicago at the end of the Great Depression. Her father was a union organizer. Her mother was also employed, and Chicago wrote in her autobiography that one of her earliest memories is of her mother dressed in a suit going off to work. Her parents played host to a network of friends who were passionate about politics and the arts. Like her mother, Chicago recalls, her parents' female friends were crucial role models, shaping her conviction that she could stake out her own future.

Devastated by father's death

Chicago began drawing when she was about three years old. From the age of eight until she left for college ten years later, she took art classes at the renowned Art Institute of Chicago. Her mother encouraged her interest and always found the money to pay for art classes. Chicago remembers her father inventing games of math and logic for her and her younger brother. He also encouraged their powers of observation with games when they traveled, which Chicago says helped her develop her skills as an artist. His death—when Judy was only 13—was devastating; she spent her teens preserving a calm exterior while experiencing guilt and anguish over his passing.

Chicago says she "escaped" to California to attend college, and, except for a year in New York in 1959, has been based there ever since. She excelled at the University of California at Los Angeles (UCLA) and became involved in art and politics, especially the growing civil rights movement. During these years Chicago sought therapy to address the emotional issues that had emerged after her father's death. The therapeutic experience provided considerable material for her later work. She married, but her husband died in an automobile accident scarcely a year after their marriage.

Miraculously, this second terrible blow had a bright side; Chicago recalls working constantly in her studio, painting images of death, rebirth, and separation. "In ... struggling to come to terms with my circumstances," she wrote, "I made myself into the artist I was always determined to be.... I learned what it meant to make art seriously."

Still, Chicago's determination ran into a large obstacle: the sexist attitudes of the art world. During and after college, she found that few men took her work or her ambitions seriously, and those who expressed interest were often making sexual advances. Gallery owners who came to the studio she shared with a male friend (who later became her second husband) would look at his work and ignore hers. At the same time, she found few women teachers or artists who could serve as role models.

Despite obstacles, mastered male-oriented skills

But art teachers, Chicago soon realized, assumed that the women in their classes had the same skills in handling materials and using tools as the men had. In truth, Chicago, like most women, had no experience with table saws, drills, and other tools; she forced herself to master these machines, many of which she had never seen before, refusing to admit that she needed help—not that any was forthcoming. "I just maintained a 'brave front' and bumbled my way through the problems," she wrote.

Having met that obstacle, Chicago went on to study several industrial processes not frequently used in art in those days. She enrolled in an auto body school to learn how to use spray paint, worked with a boat building company to learn how to handle fiberglass, and even apprenticed herself to a fireworks expert to master the creation of "environments" with smoke and light. Unfortunately, she was never able to finish her work toward a permit as a pyrotechnician—a fireworks expert—because she could not abide the sexual advances she received from her "boss." In all of these areas, Chicago was inevitably the sole woman, and she found herself the object of much harassment.

Throughout the 1960s, Chicago felt constrained by the sort of impersonal painting that seemed the only path to success, hoping secretly to pursue a more emotionally immediate direction. In the meantime, she painted competently in the **abstract** vein preferred by critics and gallery owners. The highest praise for a woman artist in those days was that she "painted like a man," wrote Chicago in her autobiography. Feeling discontented with institutionally approved creation, she periodically ventured into more personal territory. Yet work that expressed her feelings and struggles as a woman seemed to anger and intimidate viewers, particularly male ones. Teachers, critics, and gallery owners—most of them men—discouraged her at every turn.

Inspired by women's movement

The growing women's movement of the 1960s provided much-needed help and encouragement. Chicago, on reading some of the early feminist writings from the East Coast, found they expressed many of the same feelings she had about male domination and the obstacles preventing women from exploring their emotions and convictions. She realized that she was not alone in her struggles as a woman or an artist. Although it took a great deal of courage, Chicago began showing her more personal work and openly discussing the difficulties faced by female artists. Her first major step in this direction came in 1969, when she organized a show of her works at California State College in Fullerton. At this exhibit she posted a notice stating that she was giving up the name "imposed on her through male social dominance" and choosing her own, Judy Chicago.

Throughout the 1970s Chicago immersed herself in teaching, beginning a class for women artists at Fresno State College in which she encouraged her students to learn the traditionally male-oriented skills she had never been taught. Together they explored the issues surrounding the role of women in a male-dominated society and how women could transform their experiences into art. In 1972 Chicago moved this program to the new California School of the Arts—Cal Arts—where she and artist Miriam Schapiro established the first feminist art program in the country and set up a community of women artists on the West Coast. They also opened the first cooperative gallery for women artists on the West Coast. This eventually led to the establishment of the Woman's Building in Los Angeles, a bustling art center of studios, galleries, and exhibit spaces. Their most controversial project, however, was *Womanspace,* a renovated house inhabited by art students who created in it the first "all-female art environment."

Chicago also assembled the very first collection of slides of artwork made by women. Having keenly felt a lack of role models past and present, she began the critical task of researching the lives of women in art history. In addition to the arts and crafts of women of the ancient cultures of the Americas, Asia, and Africa, Chicago gathered information on women in European art, beginning with medieval nuns who worked on illuminated manuscripts. She discovered numerous prominent women painters from the 1600s through the 1900s whose work was often attributed to men.

The Dinner Party

In addition to her teaching, Chicago began in the late 1970s to produce some of her most innovative and controversial art. In 1979 she exhibited in San Francisco what is still her best-known work, *The Dinner Party*. It consists of a huge triangular table, about 48 feet long on each side, on which are placed 39 place settings, each of which features a wine goblet, cutlery, and an individually sculpted and painted china plate. These items sit on runners of white linen cloth edged in gold and embroidered using needlework techniques culled from history. Each place setting is dedicated to and describes the life of a famous woman in history. In addition, the table sits on a floor made of 2,300 handmade porcelain tiles, which are inscribed with the names of 999 other women of achievement in the same field as each of the women celebrated on the table. This elaborate work took six years to complete; Chicago wrote that she hoped it would demonstrate how "women's achievements have been repeatedly erased from the historic record."

The Dinner Party was an important milestone for several reasons—financial, political, and critical. It received no monetary support from art patrons, corporations, or any other body of the art establishment but was instead funded completely through a "grass-roots" organizing campaign, with small donations from enthusiastic supporters around the country. Chicago has continued this unusual style of fund-raising and established her own nonprofit funding organization for exhibiting and maintaining her works. *The Dinner Party* was also unique in that it was created by a group of over 400 artisans under Chicago's direction, rather than resulting from her soli-

tary effort. Chicago's interest, she says, is in making art more democratic and in encouraging women to communicate and work with each other.

The massive creation has been viewed by over a million people in six countries. Critics, however, have expressed reservations. The work's first tour was canceled, and considerable scandal erupted due to accusations of pornography; indeed, some vilified *The Dinner Party* as "tastelessly graphic" because some of its imagery has to deal with female sexuality. Chicago is accustomed to this kind of criticism and regards it as another example of male institutional reaction to female power.

The Dinner Party, 1979.
Mixed media, 48' x 48' x 48'. Copyright Judy Chicago, 1979. Photograph © Donald Woodman.

Ignited more controversy with exploration of birth

Chicago's next work, begun in 1980, was called *The Birth Project.* Her research in creation myths from around the world led her to the discovery that childbirth imagery occupies a predominant place in the history of art. Over five years, Chicago went directly to women around the country and questioned them about their experiences giving birth. She then designed approximately 100 works that comprise the project. True to her belief in democratizing art, she had the designs realized in needlework by women from around the United States, Canada, and New Zealand. Chicago says that through this project, she longed to address a subject "rich in meaning and significance for women's lives." She discovered, however, that exploring this most fundamental of human experiences caused unrest. Despite its obviously commonplace nature, the subject and its attendant imagery remain a source of discomfort for a significant portion of the culture.

In her next work, Chicago confronted another uncomfortable subject: the Holocaust. She and her third husband, Donald Woodman, became interested in this wrenching historical episode in 1985 after seeing Claude Lanzmann's epic film *Shoah,* which depicts the Nazi attempt to exterminate European Jewry. Chicago describes *The Holocaust Project* as a personal record of her quest to understand this terrible period. After two years of study, Chicago and Woodman spent several months visiting various sights in Europe. The exhibit itself was structured as a "journey into the darkness of the Holocaust and out into the light of hope." Its many elements were created with painting, photography, needlework, silkscreen, tapestry, and stained glass.

Controversy over Chicago's work has remained a constant. In 1990 she decided it was time to find a permanent home for *The Dinner Party* and offered to donate it to a new museum being built at the University of the District of Columbia. Yet the old brouhaha was reignited, and a tangle of such crucial concerns as freedom of speech, the role of local and national politics in public art, and feminist and multicultural issues led her to withdraw her offer. The tussle stressed how Chicago has succeeded in her goal of provoking dialogue and challenging boundaries, even when the resultant dialogue has failed to completely eliminate the boundaries.

Despite her reputation for challenging society's sacred cows, Chicago's works have been exhibited around the world. She is the author of several books and lectures frequently. Her work has been the subject of four documentary films. Chicago's art and feminist politics have created a new environment for women artists. She continues to inspire her audiences by painting a brighter future over the canvas of past injustice and neglect.

Masterworks

1964	*Car Hood* (sprayed acrylic lacquer on Chevrolet hood)
1966-67	*Ten Part Cylinders* (fiberglass)
1968	*Red Dome Set* (sprayed acrylic lacquer on formed acrylic)
1971	*Red Flag* (photo-lithograph)
1973	*Great Ladies Transforming Themselves into Butterflies* (sprayed acrylic on canvas)
1979	*The Dinner Party* (multimedia)

Christo

Born June 13, 1935
Gabrovo, Bulgaria

"I create gentle disturbance for a short time."

C hristo is a wrap artist, encasing buildings, bridges, islands, coastlines, and even air in drapery as varied as plastic wrap, metals, and manufactured fabrics. His large **environmental art** projects take years to plan and execute, but the finished products exist for only a few days or weeks. Christo's staged encounters between environment and fleeting alteration of that environment explore one of art's oldest themes: humanity versus nature. Yet his style has guaranteed controversy, and he has been attacked as a one-note artist, a charlatan, and even a publicity hound. Others praise him as a genius whose art is "stirring and poetic." In any case, it is undeniable that Christo has changed the role of public art and stirred debate about its relationship to the natural world.

Christo—professionally known by his first name only—was born Christo Javacheff in Bulgaria, which was occupied by the Nazis during his early childhood and then was invaded by the Soviets at the end of World War II, when the artist was about ten years old. He was the second of three sons born to

Ivan Javacheff, a chemist and businessman, and Tzveta Dimitrova, a political activist. In his late teens he studied art at the Fine Arts Academy in Sofia, the capital of Bulgaria, learning to paint in the strict **realist** style propounded by the Soviet government. He also studied art and theater in Czechoslovakia for a short time. When the Hungarian revolution broke out in 1956, Christo managed to escape to the West and studied art briefly in Vienna, Austria. After a short stay in Switzerland, he moved to Paris in 1958.

In Paris Christo met and married Jeanne-Claude Guillebon, who became his artistic and business partner, as well as photographer for many of their projects. She also serves as the organizer and administrator of their corporation, which controls the finances of these ventures. They moved to New York in 1964.

Began wrapping beer cans and wine bottles

Christo began wrapping objects for display purposes in Paris in the early 1960s. He started with small items, like beer cans and wine bottles, then moved to bicycles, road signs, and cars. He also wrapped huge piles of crates along a harbor in Cologne, Germany, and covered shop windows and corridors of shops. The origin of this approach is unclear; Christo told one writer that it may have developed when he and other art students in Sofia were "drafted" to decorate a railway embankment at the local train station. Decorating an actual location with common materials appealed to him.

Christo's projects—known as "Christos"—have grown in size over the years. Using various kinds of fabric and rope he has wrapped a medieval tower in Spoleto, Italy (1968), the city hall of Bern, Switzerland (1968), Chicago's Museum of Contemporary Art (1969), and part of the coastline near Sydney, Australia (1969). He also shrouded some islands in Biscayne Bay, Florida (1980), as well as the Pont Neuf (1985), one of the most important bridges crossing the Seine River in Paris.

Christo has also explored other media. One form of his constructions uses oil barrels, which he piles in the shape of a "mastaba," an ancient Egyptian tomb structure. His first stack

Pont Neuf Wrapped, Paris, 1985. Reproduced by permission of Reuters/Bettmann.

of oil barrels blocked the Rue Visconti in Paris in 1962. Entitled *Iron Curtain—Wall of Oil Barrels*, it was built a year before the Soviets established the "Iron Curtain" dividing East and West Germany. Most recently, Christo has planned to erect a huge oil-barrel mastaba in the Middle Eastern city of Abu Dhabi as a symbol of "the [United Arab] Emirate and of the 20th-Century oil civilization." If built, this mastaba would be larger than the Great Pyramid in Egypt.

An expert in the art of negotiation

Other Christos have involved flowing fabrics, which he calls curtains, fences, or gates. The first of these was installed in 1972; it consisted of 200,000 feet of orange nylon fabric hung as a curtain across Rifle Gap, a narrow valley near Aspen, Colorado. The local population opposed the plan at first, but Christo met with them, with local officials, and with environmentalists who raised objections. Through this and other projects, Christo has become an expert in the art of negotiation, compromise, and planning; he regards such diplomacy as part of the artwork. "For me, esthetics is everything involved in the process—the workers, the politics, the negotiations, the construction difficulty, the dealing with hundreds of people," he explained to a *New York Times* writer.

The artistic process has become more complicated over the years with each increasingly ambitious Christo project. He has worked with local, city, state, and national governments, unions, private organizations, insurance and law firms, and museum and environmental officials. In her 1990 book about Christo, Marina Vaizey wrote, "It is surprising that they [Christo and Jeanne-Claude] are not occasionally called on to give courses in the graduate business schools of the world." To be sure, it is the pair's business skills that enable them to finance these incredibly expensive projects. No public or corporate money is used for any Christo; all funds are raised through sales of drawings, books, and photographs of each project. Most of the hundreds of assistants assembling the works are volunteers.

In 1976 Christo mounted *Running Fence* in California's Sonoma and Marin counties, a 24-mile-long white fabric "fence." It meandered across the countryside, eventually trailing off into the Pacific Ocean. The project's assembly required over three years to complete, not to mention the permission of 59 landowners and 15 government agencies. The fabric was hung from steel cables strung between 2,050 steel poles embedded in the ground and stabilized with anchors and wires. As with all of Christo's projects, all parts were designed for complete removal, to leave no evidence that the project existed. Only documentation—in the form of drawings, photographs, and film—remains. While some art authorities criticized the fence as a waste of time and resources, many praised its concept and beauty. Vaizey attested, "Running Fence is ... not only a piece of sculpture ... but itself sculpts the land, and is in turn sculpted by the wind and light."

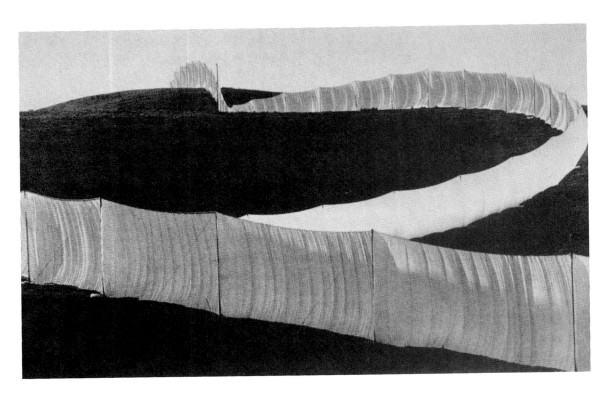

Freak wind creates tragedy of art

Indeed, because Christos exist in the open, they are affected by light, wind, and weather. These elements determine the way they appear at various times of the day and during the overall course of their existence. Such forces also occasionally raise obstacles during installation, causing design changes and delays. Once these environmental factors precipitated a tragedy. In 1991 Christo erected a project he had been planning for many years. Called *The Umbrellas, Joint Project for Japan and USA,* it consisted of thousands of blue and yellow umbrellas arrayed in a wandering line along the coasts of California and Japan. The line extended for about 12 miles in Japan and 16 in California. After exhaustive preparation, environmental studies, wind tests, and negotiations, the umbrellas were unfurled on both sides of the Pacific on the same day in October 1991. A freak gust of wind in California lifted one of the umbrellas out of its metal mooring, injuring three people and killing one. Christo was distraught and ordered all the umbrellas closed immediately. Then, in the course of dismantling the umbrellas, a Japanese worker was electrocuted as he lifted the metal poles onto a truck near a high power line.

These deaths greatly hampered Christo's work in the early 1990s, making it more difficult to convince organizations and especially insurance companies to support his projects. Nonetheless, beginning in 1993 some progress was made on what Christo has called "the project that is more important to him than all of the others put together." This endeavor, called *Wrapped Reichstag, Project for Berlin*, has been in the artist's plans for nearly 20 years. He will attempt to wrap the Reichstag, Germany's center of government and a crucially important monument in that country's history. The project faced rigid opposition for many years, but in 1993 the president of the German parliament announced that she would support the wrapping. It took another year, until February 1994, for Christo to earn the support of the parliament itself, by a vote of 292 to 223. The *New York Times* allowed that this will be "one of the most monumental [projects] in modern art history. By wrapping and unwrapping the building, Christo seeks to portray the end of an era in world history and the beginning of another." The artist plans for the project to take place in the spring of 1996.

Christo's art has been praised as a deeply meaningful series of meditations on modern life—and attacked as unimaginative and intrusive spectacle. His environmental installations are so radically contrary to traditional notions of art that they are likely to generate controversy for years to come. Christo himself, however, has no doubts about the nature of his work or his commitment to creating art for all people. He encourages dialogue about his art, the environment, and urban life and prefers

Masterworks

1962	*Iron Curtain—Wall of Oil Barrels, Paris*
1969	*Wrapped Coast, Little Bay, One Million Square Feet, Sydney, Australia*
1972	*Valley Curtain, Grand Hogback, Rifle, Colorado*
1976	*Running Fence, Marin and Sonoma counties, California*
1980	*Surrounded Islands, Biscayne Bay, Florida*
1985	*Pont Neuf Wrapped, Paris*
1991	*The Umbrellas, Joint Project for Japan and USA*

temporary works that make a bold statement to timeless icons. While making the same kinds of decisions about his work as have artists for centuries—regarding color, texture, line, and shape—he must also take into consideration matters that never concerned his predecessors, such as zoning laws, traffic, weather, and politics. "For me," Christo told the *New York Times,* "the real world involves everything: risk, danger, beauty, energy."

Salvador Dali

Born May 11, 1904
Figueras, Spain
Died January 23, 1989
Figueras, Spain

R ebel, prankster, egomaniac, genius, eccentric, virtuoso, fake—so Spanish artist Salvador Dali has been described. During his long career, he inspired as much controversy in his personal life as in his art. Indeed, the escapades that kept him in the headlines for decades affected his reputation as an artist. Yet despite all the publicity, Dali's life and thought remain mysterious. His dreamlike, often disturbing representations have had an enormous impact on modern art. A *New York Times* reviewer once wrote, "More than anyone else, he made his audience believe that nonsense could make the best sense (and the most memorable sense, too)."

Salvador Dali was born in Figueras, Spain, the son of Salvador Dali, a lawyer, and Felipa Dome Domenech. His family encouraged his early interest in art and fashioned a studio in their home for him. After attending a local school, he enrolled at the National School of Fine Arts in Madrid in 1921. His student career there mirrored his future career as an artist: though

"The only difference between me and a madman is that I am not mad."

▲ *Portrait: Reproduced by permission of AP/Wide World Photos.*

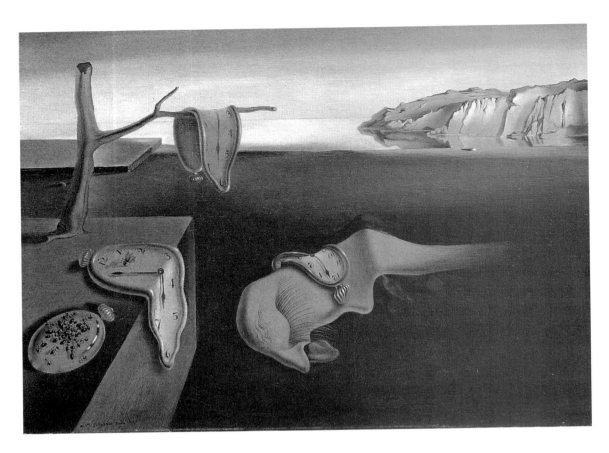

The Persistence of Memory [Persistence de la mémoire], *1931. Oil on canvas, 9½" x 13". The Museum of Modern Art, New York. Given anonymously. Photograph © 1995 The Museum of Modern Art, New York.*

recognized as a tremendous talent, he was eventually expelled as a troublemaker. He later served a short time in jail for anti-government activities. The year he was expelled from school also marked his first solo show in Madrid.

Experiments with stylistic innovation

In much of his early work, Dali experimented with **cubism** and innovative styles such as ultraism, **dadaism,** and futurism. His versatility in drawing and painting enabled him to work in a wide variety of ancient and contemporary styles. At the university Dali became associated with his countrymen poet and dramatist Federico García Lorca and filmmaker Luis Buñuel, each of whom would come to occupy an important place in modern Spanish culture.

The year 1928 was pivotal to Dali's life. It was then that he visited his fellow Spaniard and artist **Pablo Picasso** (see entry) in Paris. There he met and joined a group of artists known as the surrealists. **Surrealism** is generally thought to have begun with the publication of an article by French poet, essayist, and critic André Breton in 1924. Breton encouraged writers to delve beneath the "realistic" surface of life to explore the dreams and fantasies of the human mind. Surrealist writers and artists were profoundly influenced by the writings of the father of modern psychoanalysis, Sigmund Freud, whose theories about the unconscious mind, dreams, and sexuality rocked the Western world. Of the many well-known painters who introduced surrealism to the public, Dali was the most famous.

From 1928 to 1938 Dali painted what would prove to be his most enduring works. The best known of these, and arguably the painting most often identified with surrealism, is *The Persistence of Memory,* sometimes called *Soft Watches.* This painting typifies Dali's surrealist art, with its precise, almost

Inner Worlds of Surrealism

Surrealism did not last long as a self-contained movement, but it strongly influenced the search for meaning in modern art. Surrealist artists believed that art could reveal a world more real than the visible one. They aimed to unveil the universe of fantasy, terror, dreams, and mystery.

The French writer and critic André Breton was the first to put some of these ideas on paper in 1924. He urged writers to explore the "unconscious" mind, where dreams and fantasies are born. The method for this new kind of writing was called "automatism," or "dictation of thought without control of the mind." This meant turning off one's rational, educated mind and letting thoughts and emotions wander unencumbered. Many writers and artists explored the ideas of surrealism and automatism in the 1920s and 1930s. They also studied famed Austrian psychiatrist Sigmund Freud's writings on the unconscious mind. Surrealist groups were formed in many countries across Europe—and even in Japan.

Two main branches of surrealist painting developed in Europe: one was called "organic" or "biomorphic" surrealism. This style emphasized free-flowing—often amoeba-like—forms and highly abstract designs not representing any particular object. Artists such as Joan Miró and André Masson painted in this manner.

superrealistic style; the finest details of an impossible world are rendered impeccably. Dali carefully studied the works of the seventeenth-century Dutch artist Vermeer, who was renowned for such precision. Most of Dali's compositions are set in landscapes of exacting **Renaissance**-style **perspective,** with wide areas of deserted space receding into the distance. He was a master at lending a meticulous accuracy to his unreal scenes that made them seem somehow familiar. He called these works "hand-painted dream photographs."

Surrealism captures spirit of the times

It was only on closer inspection that viewers realized the peculiar and unsettling elements that made Dali's art more a product of nightmares than dreams: watches become soft and melt like cheese, beautiful women are propped up with crutches,

The style known as "naturalistic" surrealism or "superrealism," as seen in the paintings of Salvador Dali, Yves Tanguy, René Magritte, and others, is better known. The works of these artists was executed in an extremely realistic way, using familiar objects, recognizable scenes, and traditional perspective. The viewer generally feels comfortable with these paintings until he or she detects that something is "wrong." Exaggeration, distortion, and unexpected relationships often occur in these surrealist works. One finds teacups lined with fur, a beautiful piece of fruit so huge it threatens to push down the walls of the room containing it, or a giraffe loping across a landscape with its back on fire. There is no gravity, no comfort, and certainly no logic in these visions, yet they manage to communicate some fundamental truth about the human condition. Often it is a truth that we prefer to keep hidden in the recesses of our minds.

For centuries artists used their skills to approximate the world of nature as faithfully as they could. Many feel photography, as it developed and grew in popularity from 1850 on, usurped from artists the role of visually capturing nature and the visible world. The surrealists, on the other hand, tried to express inner, unseen landscapes. And the very act of creating became as important, if not more important, than actually communicating to an audience. This notion became a major trend in twentieth-century art.

insects smother objects, and mysterious items hatch from eggs. The paintings are rife with hidden and symbolic meanings; Dali said he painted his inner feelings of disintegration, of people surrendering to machines, and of time preying on everything. It was a message that meshed perfectly with the mood of Western culture in his day. His paintings, including *The Enigma of William Tell, Burning Giraffe,* and *Accommodations of Desire,* earned him a reputation as a highly gifted artist with a unique and totally novel message.

In the 1930s Dali's paintings were exhibited in surrealist shows in major cities in Europe and the United States. He compounded his notoriety by projecting an eccentric, rebellious image. Dali was known far and wide for his tremendous, perfectly shaped handlebar mustache, his wide, flowing capes, and his flamboyant manner. His glamour and high spirits made him popular in fashionable circles. He perfected the art of uttering

The Sacrament of the Last Supper, *1956. Reproduced by permission of AP/Wide World Photos.*

outrageous statements designed to shock, lavishing particular attention on the art world.

Collaborates with Buñuel on films

Dali was not just a painter; he also explored writing, book illustration, stage design, and fashion and jewelry design. His most respected work outside of painting is his collaboration with Buñuel on two films, *Un Chien Andalou* (1928) and *L'Age d'Or* (1931). These contain much of the same troubling imagery that appears in Dali's paintings. Both are considered classics.

During World War II Dali and his wife, Gala Eluard, moved to the United States. There the painter's showy lifestyle and love of publicity gained him greater repute than did his art. He was frequently reported engaging in scandalous behavior in trendy Hollywood or New York City locales. Once he crashed through the window of a Fifth Avenue gallery to rearrange a display of his work. He was often criticized for pulling such stunts just for the notices he'd receive in the press; some suggested he had little left to say in his art and had become a mere celebrity.

In the late 1940s Dali began creating art for the Catholic Church, painting traditional subjects on a grand scale. While several critics deemed these works bland, many enjoyed the opportunity to share Dali's view of New Testament events. In his later years he turned to the pursuit of science in his art, experimenting with three-dimensional images and holograms. Sadly, the myth he built around himself compromised the seriousness with which his work was regarded. Whether or not he himself came to believe the myth of his persona is unclear. At one point he was accused of signing blank sheets of paper—reportedly thousands per day—so that either he or someone else could add a drawing to the paper and sell it at a high price, as it bore his valuable signature. Many such occurrences were blamed on the people who controlled his business affairs toward the end of his life, when his health was in marked decline.

In his twenties and thirties Dali was a pioneering artist who perfected a truly modern style. The many exhibits mounted during his lifetime demonstrate the sheer quantity of work he produced. In 1980 the Pompidou Center in Paris exhibited 168 paintings, 219 drawings, 38 objects, roughly 2,000 documents, and a specially built "Dali environment." Another large show was presented in Madrid in 1983. And two museums were built to hold his works, one in St. Petersburg, Florida, the other in his hometown of Figueras, Spain. Though controversy followed him throughout his life, the creative vision Dali expressed through surrealism cemented his place in modern art.

Masterworks

1929	*Illumined Pleasures*
	Accommodations of Desire
1931	*The Persistance of Memory*
	Slumber
	Burning Giraffe
1935	*Portrait of Gala and "The Angelus" by Millet*
	Soft Construction with Boiled Beans (Premonition of Civil War)
1946	*The Temptation of St. Anthony*

Stuart Davis

Born December 7, 1894
Philadelphia, Pennsylvania

Died June 24, 1964
New York, New York

"I am an American. I studied art in America. I paint what I see in America, in other words, the American Scene."

From the 1920s to the 1960s Stuart Davis was one of the top painters on the U.S. art scene. He belonged to no particular school or movement but developed his own unique style, which one writer dubbed "jazzy American Cubism." Davis—who claimed to take "all of American contemporary life" as his subject matter—used geometric shapes, bright colors, and the rhythms of music, especially jazz, in his paintings and murals. He was one of the first artists to use lettering, numbers, and the labels of products like cigarettes and cleansers in his works. His paintings are often recognizable by the incorporation of his signature into the design. Davis's work exercised an important influence on American artists of the 1940s, 1950s, and 1960s.

Art was at the center of Davis's upbringing. His mother, Helen Stuart Folke, attended the Pennsylvania Academy of Fine Arts, where she met and married fellow student Edward Wyatt Davis. When their eldest son, Stuart, was born in 1894, Edward Davis was working as the art editor of a local newspaper; he had, among other duties, the job of hiring the "quick-sketch artists" who illustrated the paper. Four men who worked for him in Philadelphia went on to establish an important movement in art called the Ashcan School. The young Stuart Davis knew these men and their work.

Left high school to study in New York

When Davis was about eight years old, his father took a new job with a newspaper in Newark, New Jersey, not far from New York City. The family moved to a town nearby where Davis went to school until he was 15. He left high school after one year, traveling to New York to study art at a new school opened by artist Robert Henri. Henri was a leader of the Ashcan School, so named because the artists associated with it portrayed scenes of city life, incorporating saloons, slums, and street people. Traditionalists considered these improper subjects for art and scorned Henri as a radical teacher because he encouraged his students to wander New York City with their sketch pads and record "real life."

While touring the neighborhoods of New York, Davis became entranced by the rhythms, colors, and energy of urban life, which are evident in many of his paintings. He often visited the bars and clubs where African American musicians played jazz. "For a number of years jazz had a tremendous influence on my thoughts about art and life," he told an interviewer in 1960.

Near the end of his three years of study with Henri, Davis began producing illustrations for such magazines as *Harper's Bazaar* and *The Masses.* He set up his own studio in New York, inviting critics to review his paintings. At 18, he was one of the youngest artists ever to exhibit works in the International Exhibit of Modern Art, which was held in a huge armory building in New York in February 1913. Davis called the Armory Show, as it came to be known, the most decisive moment in his career—thanks not to the display of his own paintings, but to the work of other artists he saw there. This was the first time the creations of **Pablo Picasso, Paul Gauguin, Henri Matisse** (see entries), and other modern European painters were shown in the United States. Davis was astonished by these artists' use of color

◀ *Portrait (p. 96): Self-portrait, 1919.* Oil on canvas, 22¼" x 18¼". Courtesy Amon Carter Museum, Fort Worth, Texas.

purely for design and their experimentation with new ways of rendering (or ignoring) **perspective**. Davis wrote in his autobiography that seeing these works gave him "the same kind of excitement I got from the numerical precisions of ... piano players in the Negro saloons, and I resolved that I would quite definitely have to become a 'modern' artist."

Painted *Lucky Strike*

Of all the styles to which Davis was exposed at the show, **cubism** was of preeminent importance. He spent the next 15 years working out its ideas and theories—as well as those of **fauvism, expressionism, dadaism,** and **surrealism**—in his paintings. He spent time painting in towns along the coast of Massachusetts, in Cuba (while recovering from the flu), and in New York. During World War I he served briefly in the army, drawing maps and charts. After the war he experimented with the ideas of cubist **collage.** In 1921 he painted *Lucky Strike,* considered a landmark of his career; it is comprised of geometric shapes, letters, and numbers he saw on a package of cigarettes. Although he modeled his canvas on a real object, Davis was getting closer to making truly **abstract art**, that is, work that does not attempt to "represent" anything outside of itself.

In the late 1920s Davis spent a full year concentrating on painting one subject, trying to purify his vision into absolutely flat, abstract shapes. These paintings were known as the "Eggbeater Series" because Davis's "subject" was a **still life** of an eggbeater, a rubber glove, and an electric fan. He painted these over and over again until the objects disappeared and his paintings revealed only the relationships among line, plane, and color. After this year of intense theoretical study and painting, Davis sailed to Paris with his friend Bessie Chosak; the two later married in the French capital. For roughly a year and a half, Davis painted scenes of the streets and cafés of Paris. His work from this period, such as *Place Pasdeloup,* is characterized by his energetic use of decorative lines, loops, and squiggles.

Davis returned to New York in the early 1930s to face the economic nightmare of the Great Depression. Like many artists

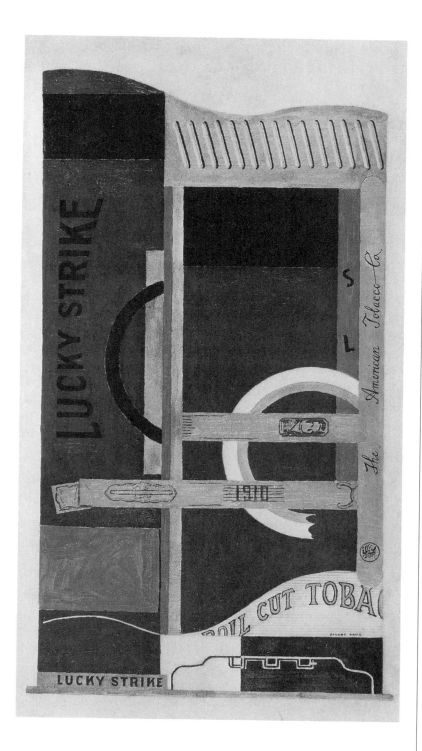

Lucky Strike, *1921. Oil on canvas, 33¼" x 18". The Museum of Modern Art, New York. Gift of the American Tobacco Company. Photograph © 1995 The Museum of Modern Art, New York.*

of the time, he became involved in liberal political causes and was active in the Artists' Union. His most familiar works from the 1930s are his **mural** paintings, many of them sponsored by the Federal Art Project. In 1932 he painted a mural for the men's room at Rockefeller Center in New York. He called it *Mural (Men without Women)* and used mostly black and white paint to create abstracted shapes of pipes, barber poles, and cigars. Another mural, *Swing Landscape,* was originally painted for a housing project and was described by one writer as "a massive jigsaw puzzle of bright-colored shapes through which the elements of a cityscape are discernible." Davis also painted a mural for radio station WNYC, illustrating his love of jazz with depictions of instruments and musical symbols. Like the painter **Piet Mondrian** (see entry), who came to the United States in the 1940s and was inspired by modern music, Davis felt that "jazz was the only thing that corresponded to an authentic art in America."

In 1932 Davis's wife died; six years later he married Roselle Springer, an artist who shared his love of jazz. They named their son Earl after pianist Earl "Fatha" Hines.

Inspired by skyscrapers, taxis, electric signs

By the 1940s Davis began to achieve recognition as a major force in a new, distinctively American form. He claimed to have been inspired by the things he saw in New York and around the country, some of which he enumerated in a 1943 article for *Art News,* among them "American wood and iron work, skyscrapers, taxis, chain-store fronts, fast travel by train, car, and plane, electric signs, brilliant colors on gas stations, movies and radio, and the music of J. S. Bach and Earl Hines." Davis did not actually illustrate these typically twentieth-century American phenomena; instead, they helped to determine the tempo, colors, and design of his creations. This can be seen in such energetic 1940s and 1950s works as *Rapt at Rappaport's* and *Mellow Pad.* He used lettering and numbers in his paintings to reflect the proliferation of billboards and neon signs on the American landscape. Davis's titles are frequently witty, full of

alliteration and American slang: *Composition Concrete, Tropes de Teens, Colonial Cubism,* and *Blips and Ifs.*

In the 1950s excitement over new styles such as **abstract expressionism** and action painting somewhat eclipsed Davis's work. He nonetheless continued to pursue his muse, showing his paintings in numerous exhibitions during the last 20 years of his life. He mounted a solo retrospective show in Venice, Italy, in 1952, as well as solo exhibits in San Francisco and at the Whitney Museum of American Art in New York. His paintings were included in group shows in Mexico (1958) and Moscow (1959) and toured many European cities in 1955. The many honors bestowed upon Davis include two Guggenheim International Awards, the Fine Arts Gold Medal of the American Insti-

The Barber Shop.
Reproduced by permission of the Bettmann Archive.

Stuart Davis

Masterworks

1921	*Lucky Strike*
1924	*Untitled (Odol)*
1927	*Eggbeater Number 1*
1928	*Rue Vercingetorix*
1932	*Mural (Men without Women)*
1938	*Swing Landscape*
1945	*Mellow Pad*
1952	*Rapt at Rappaport's*
1954	*Colonial Cubism*
1963-64	*Blips and Ifs*

tute of Architecture, and the Temple Gold Medal of the Pennsylvania Academy of Fine Arts (where his parents had met).

Art scholars, historians, and critics have long engaged in vigorous debate as to whether Stuart Davis can be considered a "father" of the 1960s **pop art** movement. Certainly the pop artists found inspiration in packaging materials, signs, and lettering. One writer points out that the difference between them and Davis is one of attitude: Davis found contemporary American life, including advertising and consumer products, exciting and colorful—a proper subject for art, while the pop artists used these elements to comment—most often negatively—on American society and consumerism.

In the early 1990s museums in New York and San Francisco hung a large retrospective exhibit of Davis's works to commemorate the one-hundredth anniversary of his birth. His paintings still reflect the excitement he felt about an America that was vibrant, growing, and modern. As a *New York Herald Tribune* critic wrote in 1960, "Davis's abstractions are like fireworks that never go out."

Marcel Duchamp

Born July 28, 1887
Blainville, France
Died October 2, 1968
Neuilly-sur-Seine, France

Marcel Duchamp remains an enigmatic and unclassifiable figure in art history. He painted for only a short time and was never really a sculptor in the conventional sense. Indeed, he claimed to be "anti-art," and despite an unusual and controversial career in the art world, he preferred to play chess. Despite all this—or perhaps because of it—he has emerged as a critical influence on numerous twentieth-century art movements. Duchamp wanted the art world to throw off its old "chains" and pursue an "imaginative adventure."

The Duchamp family lived a prosperous life near Rouen, in the Normandy region of France, and produced several artists: four of Eugène and Lucie Nicolle Duchamp's six children followed the muse. The eldest, Gaston, became a reputable painter under the name Jacques Villon. The second in line, Raymond, known as Raymond Duchamp-Villon, was one of the first cubist sculptors. He seemed to have a successful career in front of him when he was killed in World War I. The fourth child,

"Once the artist makes something, it gains recognition through the intervention of the spectator. I consider the viewer just as important as the maker."

Suzanne, also became a painter, but the family member who made the biggest mark was the third, Marcel.

Marcel Duchamp enjoyed a happy childhood, attending local schools and taking up drawing at an early age. His older brothers went to Paris to become artists when he was still very young, and their example influenced him greatly; he joined them in Paris when he was 17. Eugène provided each of them with a living allowance while they developed their careers. Duchamp studied at an art school but found it uninspiring, preferring to spend his time playing billiards. After about a year, he volunteered for the military service but was rejected for medical reasons. He worked as a librarian for a time.

Exhausts styles of the day to blaze trail

When Duchamp returned to Paris in 1906 he began painting in a manner similar to the wild, colorful style known as **fauvism** and also experimented with many of the ideas of French painter **Paul Cézanne** (see entry). One of his paintings from this time, *The Chess Players,* evokes a genial mood through the use of vivid colors. In the few years between roughly 1906 and 1910, Duchamp experimented with and mastered most of the prevailing styles; he then moved on, restless to find his own form of expression. It was during this time that Spanish painter **Pablo Picasso** (see entry) and Frenchman Georges Braque were introducing the ideas of **cubism** to the art world, and their flattened approach to space and simultaneous employment of a variety of perspectives greatly appealed to Duchamp. He painted several works in the cubist style, including *Portrait of Chess Players.* This painting, done just a year after *The Chess Players,* marked a decided stylistic departure. Using cubist ideas, Duchamp fragmented the figures in the scene, favored muted colors, and emphasized the two-dimensional surface of the picture.

But Duchamp soon grew restless with cubism, which he ultimately found too static for his purposes. He longed to bring action and motion to his canvases. Inspired by developments in photography and film, Duchamp began to depict repeated forms—usually human figures—overlapping across the canvas to convey the energy of motion. The geometric attributes of cubism made Duchamp's figures appear to metamorphose into machines. One writer ventured that the figures in these early paintings seemed "in acceleration towards lift-off."

When Duchamp showed what would be his most renowned work in this style—*Nude Descending a Staircase*—at an exhibition in Paris in 1911, he was asked to take it down. A later version was displayed at the famous Armory Show in New York City in 1913, a massive exhibition that included numerous creations thought shocking and scandalous at the time. Duchamp's *Nude* was the most brazen of all. One critic wrote that it looked like "an explosion in a brick factory." Part of the outrage was due to the title, which, combined with this particular imagery, violated the unwritten rule that nudes were soft, luminous figures in ideal landscapes; Duchamp had the nerve to present what looked like a mechanical figure walking down a flight of stairs. Critics said Duchamp's painting was a symbol of "the insanity to which modern art had progressed." Duchamp enjoyed outraging these conservatives and snubbing their "dead" art; his reputation as a rebel was established in a single stroke.

Duchamp continued in this vein during these early years and produced, among other works, a series of drawings and paintings using chess pieces and based on the idea of speed and action. In *The King and Queen Surrounded by Swift Nudes,* the chess pieces seem in the process of being blasted to bits by powerful winds that sweep across the scene. Duchamp also became consumed with mechanical apparatuses, studying and experimenting with ideas of motion and rotation. His *Bicycle Wheel* mounted on a stool is considered the forerunner of **kinetic art** and the mobiles of **Alexander Calder** (see entry). In fact, it was Duchamp who coined the term "mobiles" when he saw Calder's moving sculptures in the 1930s.

Invents outrageous "Readymades"

In keeping with his renegade aesthetic outlook, Duchamp also created a new art object called the "Readymade," predicated on his conviction that anything could be a work of art; the determination simply depended on who made it. Some of Duchamp's

NU DESCENDANT UN ESCALIER

Readymades may have been largely a joke at the traditional art world's expense, though subsequent generations would find their conceptual basis a source of liberation. One of Duchamp's early Readymades was a snow shovel he bought at a hardware store, signed and hung from the ceiling. He titled it *In Advance of the Broken Arm.* He also bought a cheap print of a landscape scene, added two dots of red and green paint, and called it *Pharmacy.* One Readymade caused a great scandal when Duchamp tried to enter it in an exhibit in New York in 1917. The work was called *Fountain;* it was a white porcelain urinal signed on the front by "R. Mutt." The exhibition committee rejected this creation, but Duchamp's refutation of their decision provides something of a Readymade manifesto: "Whether Mr. Mutt with his own hands made the fountain or not has no importance," Duchamp claimed in an article. "He CHOSE it. He took an ordinary article of life, placed it so that its useful significance disappeared under a new title and point of view—[he] created a new thought for that object." The question "What is art?," a primary concern of Duchamp's, became crucial to many of the movements that followed him, particularly **dadaism** and **pop art.**

Duchamp's most famous Readymade was a print of the *Mona Lisa* by the Italian **Renaissance** master **Leonardo da Vinci** (see entry). Duchamp added a mustache and beard to the woman's face and gave it the nonsensical title *L.H.O.O.Q.* It is interesting that Duchamp chose to use Leonardo's work for one of his Readymades, since his interest in physics, math, and engineering have led some to compare him to Leonardo. Both looked to science and philosophy for ideas and freedom from the constraints of mainstream art. Leonardo refined the use of **perspective**, providing a formal template for the creation of spatial illusion. Duchamp decided that, several centuries after Leonardo, the illusion of three-dimensional space had been fully explored. He wanted to take art into the fourth dimension.

These concepts swirled around Duchamp between about 1912 and 1923. He regarded his Readymades and other pieces as

◀ Nude Descending a Staircase, No. 2, *1912. Approx. 58" x 35". Philadelphia Museum of Art. Louise and Walter Arensberg Collection. Reproduced by permission of Bridgeman/Art Resource, NY.*

mere diversions and had dedicated himself to the creation of a masterpiece that would reveal art as "a system of visual events in space." He labored diligently during these years, absorbed in calculating, planning, studying, and sketching. Unlike many other artists, Duchamp was not so much interested in *creating* art as he was in using art to demonstrate his ideas and theories. The end product of all this appeared in 1923 under the title *The Bride Stripped Bare by Her Bachelors, Even.* It is a nine-foot-high installation constructed of drawn and painted objects pressed between two panes of glass. This *Large Glass,* as it is often called, is only the visible portion of the work; Duchamp considered the 93 documents that describe the work, published as *The Green Box,* as important as the glass itself.

The Bride Stripped Bare by Her Bachelors, Even

Calvin Tomkins, in his book on Duchamp, instructed, "Before venturing into the strange and marvelous country of Duchamp's *Large Glass,* the explorer [needs] ... good eyesight, a lively imagination and a certain familiarity with the development of modern art." Like many creations, this enigmatic artifact can really only "work" when it is viewed in real life where it hangs at the Philadelphia Museum of Art. The various images—the bachelors, a chocolate grinder, a tie, a toboggan, weights, splashes of liquid—embedded between the glass panes refer to objects from Duchamp's childhood, some prosaic and some mystical, and suggest his ideas about sexuality and scientific concepts, as well as his often obscure sense of humor. Taken as a whole, the piece functions like a map of Duchamp's imagination. The *Large Glass* cannot be looked *at* without also being looked *through,* so viewers see its environment as part of the work. Since these surroundings—including the light in the room and the movement of people—change over time, Duchamp can be seen to have successfully integrated some of his ideas about the fourth dimension, or time itself, into the work.

In 1923, after working for many years on his masterpiece, Duchamp abandoned it and appeared to abandon the creation of artifacts in general. Of the *Large Glass,* he said, "I had lost interest, it no longer concerned me." He considered it unfinished until an accident several years later. Part of the glass was shattered when it was being moved in preparation for its first exhibition in 1926; since this intrusion of chance added another dimension to the work, Duchamp declared it finished.

Art or Junk?

"Is it art or junk?," one journalist asked rhetorically after seeing the works displayed at the 1913 International Exhibition of Modern Art in New York City. The show was such a huge undertaking that no formal exhibition space of adequate size could be found. The organizers resorted to renting the 69th Infantry Regiment Armory, a huge castle-like structure; thus the 1913 modern art exhibition became known as the Armory Show.

Once inside, few cared about the location since their heads were spinning from what they saw. No single event has had such an impact on American art. The work of most of the important European artists of the time was practically unknown in the United States; though only about one-third of the 1,600 works on display were by European

artists, these received by far the most attention and criticism. Works by **Vincent van Gogh, Paul Gauguin, Pablo Picasso, Paul Cézanne, Constantin Brancusi,** and **Henri Matisse** (see entries) absolutely stunned and outraged the large crowds and critics. These pioneers, though respected in Europe, were met in America by great hostility.

The new style of cubism elicited perhaps the loudest disdain. "Cubists and Futurists are making insanity pay," read the headline in the *New York Times*. Reviewers slung terms like "immoral," "indecent," and "nasty" at the exhibit's groundbreaking creations. The room in which the cubist works were hung was called "the chamber of horrors." The furor even provoked debate about whether children and pregnant women should be barred from attending the show. Modern audiences may have difficulty un-

After 1923 Duchamp devoted much of his time to playing chess, becoming so proficient that he competed in various championships. Eventually he owned a collection of chess sets made by his friends, many of the most famous artists of the time, including Francis Picabia, **Man Ray** (see entry), and Alexander Calder. He spent most of his time in New York and Paris. In 1928 he married Lydie Sarazin-Levassor, who was considerably younger than he; the marriage lasted only a few months. Although he created no art in these years, he never stopped writing, theorizing, or participating in the art world.

Influence continues to reverberate

Duchamp's presence and ideas were important to the development of several styles in the 1920s and 1930s, notably

derstanding the outrage provoked by paintings like Cézanne's *Blue Nude* and Marcel Duchamp's *Nude Descending a Staircase*. But art that dared to question cherished aesthetic ideals was provocation indeed—an assault on the senses that seemed to mock not only the viewer, but all that the viewer held sacred.

The importance of the Armory Show can be traced in several directions. First, it was a stimulus to the community of American artists, many of whom felt behind the times after seeing these strange and exciting new works. The traditional **realism** that was popular seemed staid next to these daring innovations. A sizable group of artists was inspired by the show to travel to Europe to study. Some, like **Stuart Davis** (see entry), were moved to change their styles completely in pursuit of more modern ideas. A portion of the show traveled to Boston and Chicago after New York, and large crowds assembled in all three cities. The immense and diverse audiences—along with the dissemination of catalogues, postcards, and many newspaper and magazine articles—meant that images of modern art reached a huge number of people, thus creating a new market for it in the United States. Galleries and private collectors began accumulating challenging contemporary works. Many of these later became the foundations of museum collections around the country. Ultimately, the Armory Show's lasting influence vindicated the convictions of the painters, sculptors, and other visionaries who upset the *status quo* in art. In retrospect, the defenders of normalcy seem absurd, while the absurdists lit the way to the future.

dadaism and **surrealism.** He exercised a substantial influence on Man Ray in New York during World War I. Along with their friend Picabia, the two iconoclasts are generally considered the founders of dadaism in the United States. Duchamp also advised dealers and collectors on purchases. He traveled extensively, setting up exhibits in galleries and museums in the United States and Europe, many of them showcasing surrealist art. He also worked on film projects during these years and made some small sculptures and Readymade-type works.

In 1943 Duchamp moved to New York, where he lived for the remainder of his life. In 1954 he married Alexina Sattler and acquired a new family in her three children. Much of the art world believed him finished with painting, but he had begun in the mid-1940s to work on what would become his last major work, *Given.* He worked on this canvas quietly for

Masterworks

Paintings

1910	*The Chess Players*
1911	*Portrait of Chess Players*
1912	*The King and Queen Surrounded by Swift Nudes*
	Nude Descending a Staircase, No. 2
1923	*The Bride Stripped Bare by Her Bachelors, Even*

Objects

1913	*Bicycle Wheel*
1915	*In Advance of the Broken Arm*
1917	*Fountain*
1919	*L.H.O.O.Q*
1966	*Pocket Chess Set with Rubber Glove*

roughly 20 years; it was not made public until after his death.

Perhaps even more significant than his works was Duchamp's reputation in the last 40 years of his life; he became a legend among progressive artists. As John Canaday observed in the *New York Times,* "Marcel Duchamp has been the most destructive artist in history. At the same time and for the same reason, he has been the most influential in the adventurous course of modern art except Picasso." Duchamp's suspicion of the classical concept of art was especially influential on young American artists of the 1950s as they questioned the place of art in the age of technology and consumerism. Writings about Duchamp's work inevitably include references to later artists involved in **abstract expressionism, op art,** and **pop art** who absorbed his ideas and developed them as major innovations. It almost seems as if Duchamp's mind was too fertile for him to develop all of his ideas; his primary concern was to puncture the traditional ideas that obstructed innovation. Thus Canaday's description of him as "destructive." Duchamp uprooted and challenged ideas and techniques that had developed in Western art over hundreds, if not thousands, of years, planting the seeds of new concepts that, many years after his death, have just begun to take root.

Albrecht Dürer

Born May 21, 1471
Nuremberg, Germany
Died April 6, 1528
Nuremberg, Germany

lbrecht Dürer was the most important German artist of his time—and perhaps of all time. His love of art, science, and mathematics and his extensive travels around Europe brought him the respect and admiration of many, from the townsfolk of his native city to scholars and kings. He was the first Western artist to keep records of his financial dealings and travels and to write an autobiography, so historians have an unusually accurate picture of his life. While his oil paintings and watercolors received considerable acclaim, his place in history was ensured by his engravings and **woodcuts,** arguably the finest work ever done in the form. The latter marked another forward-looking aspect of Dürer's creativity; they permitted him to make affordable reproductions of his works and thus achieve a broader audience.

Albrecht Dürer was the son of a prosperous Nuremberg goldsmith, also named Albrecht Dürer, and Barbara Holper Dürer, whose father was also a goldsmith. At about six years of age the boy began attending school; as soon as he learned to

"Great mastership ... is only attained by much toil, labor, and expenditure of time."

▲ *Portrait:* Self-portrait, 1498. Oil on wood, 20½"x16½". Museo del Prado, Madrid. Reproduced by permission of Alinari/Art Resource, NY.

read and write his father taught him the trade of goldsmithing—he learned how to use sharp and precise cutting tools to engrave designs on metal. Young Dürer seemed to have an immediate talent for this fastidious work, but he preferred drawing and painting. When he was 13 he drew a portrait of himself looking in a mirror. This is the first of several existing self-portraits; they chronicle not only Dürer's changing visage but also his evolving technique.

Near Dürer's home lived a boy named Willibald Pirckheimer who was Dürer's friend throughout his life. Pirckheimer's father, one of the city's wealthiest residents, owned an extensive library; Dürer often borrowed its books so he could study and copy the illustrations. Both boys were very intelligent and quick-witted, and they spent countless hours over the course of their lives discussing art, politics, and issues of the day. In later years Pirckheimer financed some of Dürer's travels around Europe.

Learns to carve woodblocks

By the time he reached 15, Dürer had summoned the courage to tell his father that he wanted to be an artist. Despite his disappointment at not having his son take up the goldsmithing trade, Dürer senior agreed to apprentice the boy to a well-known artist in the city. For three years Dürer lived in the artist's household, executing various chores and learning how to paint, as well as how to carve illustrations onto wood blocks for printing. Dürer demonstrated both aptitude and enthusiasm for these endeavors; he learned quickly and spent as much time as he could walking around Nuremberg and sketching. He also endured a fair measure of teasing and abuse from the other apprentices, who were probably jealous of his talent. One of Dürer's earliest paintings from this time was a portrait of his father dressed in a fur cap and fur-lined coat; it shows the attention to detail for which Dürer would become famous.

In 1490, at the age of 18, Dürer set out on the first of his many travels, staying abroad for four years. His first stop was in the town of Colmar, Germany, where he sought the famous illustrator Martin Schongauer. But Schongauer had died just before Dürer's arrival; his family and students, however, took Dürer in and taught him the fine art of wood-block illustration for which the late illustrator was renowned. By carving his art into the blocks, the artist could make multiple prints of each picture and sell the reproductions at a low price. Dürer was a perfectionist, insisting that each line and dot of his drawings be exact; he stayed for two years in Colmar and then set out for Basel, Switzerland, to work as an illustrator for a book publisher. He did not stay in the city for long, opting instead to continue his travels around Germany and Switzerland, meeting artists and selling his drawings.

Dürer returned home to Nuremberg when he was 23 and married Agnes Frey, the daughter of his father's colleague; he also resumed his friendship with Willibald Pirckheimer and spent many hours at his home meeting the scholars and writers who gathered there. At Pirckheimer's urging, Dürer planned a trip to Italy to study the works of the Italian **Renaissance.** In the fall of 1494 he traveled to Venice, stopping at many cities and towns on the way. He enjoyed the city's social life as well as its artistic community and returned home six months later with a bevy of new concepts and approaches. His watercolor landscapes from this period are saturated with rich hues; Dürer's most famous work in this medium is *Young Hare,* in which every detail of the animal—down to the individual whiskers—is faithfully drawn. Still, beyond the realistic depiction of the image is a beauty and warmth that allows the rendering to come alive; the artist's paintings of trees and flowers share this quality.

Engraves *Four Horsemen of the Apocalypse*

During the next few years, Dürer focused on earning a living from his art. He concentrated on creating **engravings,** drawings etched into metal plates with sharp tools; like woodblocks, these plates were then spread with ink, and prints were made on a printing press. Dürer was a master of these engravings: with extremely fine lines and intricate shading, he conveyed the most minute details. The series of engravings titled *The Apocalypse*— based on writings about the end of the world by the Christian

Young Hare, *1502. Water-*
color. Albertina, Vienna.
Reproduced by permission
of Foto Marburg/Art
Resource, NY.

saint John the Divine—contains what are perhaps Dürer's mas-
terworks in the form. In *The Four Horsemen of the Apoca-*
lypse, arguably the standout print from this series, Dürer envi-
sions War, Sickness, Hunger, and Death as skeletons on horse-

back; the grandeur and grotesquerie of this image make it a touchstone in the depiction of evil, one regularly appropriated by twentieth-century popular culture.

Dürer was among the very first artists to make prints that neither served religious purposes—such as illustrations for the Bible or devotional items—nor illustrated a literary work; his engravings could be enjoyed on their own terms, a bold notion at the time. Dürer also pioneered the concept of marketing his art to a wide audience. His mother and wife often maintained a booth at the city market selling his prints, and he contracted a servant to travel around the continent dealing his prints. Up to then artwork had most often been commissioned, or ordered, by patrons or the Church; affording people of moderate means the opportunity to buy art prints at a reasonable price was quite revolutionary.

Dürer ensured that buyers knew they were acquiring his prints by signing them with his brand mark, a square-looking A with a D underneath the crossbar that is widely recognized around the world even today. But as his reputation spread, even this distinguishing feature didn't prevent certain unscrupulous entrepreneurs from trying to cash in on his success by selling fake Dürers. In 1512 the Nuremberg city council was forced to issue a decree to prohibit the selling of fakes.

Receives commissions from nobles and emperors

In 1496 Dürer received his first commission for a portrait; he was enlisted to depict the Duke of Saxony, known as Frederick the Wise, who had been impressed by Dürer's engravings. The finished work pleased the duke so much that he hired Dürer to create two paintings for a church. This was the beginning of a successful career of commissions from churches, wealthy merchants, and nobles such as Maximilian I, Emperor of Germany, and his successor, Charles V. Maximilian's admiration for Dürer was so great that in 1515 he granted the artist an annuity, or annual payment, for life. Dürer worked on a vast range of special projects for Maximilian, including a beau-

tifully illustrated prayer book and a huge wood-block print—over 12 feet high and made from 192 wood blocks—to glorify the emperor's reign; the work featured a triumphal arch and scenes from the emperor's life.

In 1505 Dürer received a commission to paint an altarpiece for a church in Venice. He spent two years there, working on the painting and immersing himself once again in the exciting city. At first the Italian painters displayed jealousy of Dürer, but by the time he was ready to return home he had earned the respect of nearly everyone with whom he'd worked and was even offered an annuity to stay in Venice. The Italians were not alone in their appreciation of Dürer's work; his prints were studied in Spain, and that country's missionaries brought some of his creations to the New World. Later Spanish artists, including Zurburan, **El Greco,** and **Francisco Goya** (see entries), were significantly influenced by his work.

The years 1520 and 1521 were filled with travel for Dürer and his wife, who journeyed extensively in Germany and Holland on their way to Antwerp, a busy port city in Belgium. Dürer's fame was such that everywhere he visited he was honored with banquets, gifts, and parties. In Antwerp Dürer met with a large group of the period's leading artists and intellectuals, including Erasmus, the Dutch scholar and theologian, and Thomas of Bologna, a student of the Italian Renaissance painter Raphael. The artists also attended the coronation of Charles V.

Nearly drowns

Toward the end of his visit to Antwerp, Dürer heard that a whale had been washed ashore in a nearby town; his substantial interest in animals moved him to travel to the site. By the time he got there, the mammal had been washed out to sea, but Dürer joined a boatload of people and sailed out to see it. A fierce, stormy wind blew up and almost capsized the small

◀ Knight, Death, and Devil, *1513. Engraving. Reproduced by permission of Giraudon/Art Resource, NY.*

Masterworks

1484	*Self-portrait* (silver point drawing)
1490	*Portrait of Dürer's Father* (oil painting)
1494	*Innsbruck Seen from the North* (watercolor)
1496	*Prodigal Son* (engraving)
1498	*Four Horsemen of the Apocalypse* (woodcut)
1500	*Self-portrait* (oil painting)
1502	*Young Hare* (watercolor)
1504	*Adam and Eve* (engraving)
1508	*Hands of an Apostle* (drawing)
1513	*Knight, Death, and Devil* (engraving)
1518	*Great Triumphal Car of Maximilian I* (woodcut)
1526	*The Four Apostles* (oil painting)

boat. Most of the passengers managed to make their way to a larger boat that came up alongside, but Dürer, the captain, and four other passengers were blown back out to sea when the mooring broke. With great difficulty, they put up a makeshift sail and floated weakly to shore. This experience left Dürer exhausted, and he came down with a fever and a "curious illness" that recurred several times in the next few years.

The 1520s were a prosperous time for Dürer. He was commissioned to do a portrait of the King of Denmark and began work on his autobiography and three other books: *Instruction in Measurement, Treatise on Fortification,* and *Treatise on Proportion.* These were intended as parts of a larger volume on the science of painting. Although Dürer was never able to complete the larger project, his enormous wealth of knowledge is apparent from the notebooks he left behind. These writings were among the first such compositions in German—most writings were in Latin at that time—and thus Dürer contributed to the development of the written vernacular, or language of the common people. The books were translated into a multitude of languages and served the teaching of art for over one hundred years. Artists such as Flemish painter **Peter Paul Rubens,** master of the Italian Renaissance **Michelangelo,** and Francisco Pacheco, teacher of Spanish court painter **Diego Velazquez** (see entries), used Dürer's texts.

In 1526 Dürer presented the city of Nuremberg with two painted panels featuring massive figures of the four apostles of Jesus, which soon hung prominently in the city hall. These panels were his last large works; the illness that first attacked him after his boating accident recurred with increasing frequency from about 1526 on. He continued to work but became progressively weaker and finally died in 1528 at the age of 55.

Dürer left behind roughly one hundred paintings, over a thousand drawings, and hundreds of woodcuts and engravings, comprising a body of work that has been the object of reverent study ever since. Fittingly, he was the first Western artist to be celebrated with a public monument—a bronze statue of his likeness stands in a plaza bearing his name in Nuremberg. It was the last of many firsts.

Helen Frankenthaler

Born December 12, 1928
New York, New York

"What concerns me when I work is not whether the picture is a landscape, or whether it's pastoral, or whether somebody will see a sunset in it. What concerns me is—did I make a beautiful picture?"

Beauty was perhaps not the primary concern of painters in the 1940s and 1950s, when Helen Frankenthaler was a young artist. While working in the bold, movement-based styles of the time, Frankenthaler developed a new technique of painting that allowed her to express emotions through the use of color, light, and space. The soak-stain technique, as her approach was known, proved influential in the ensuing decades. In 1989 a writer for the *New York Times* called Frankenthaler "the country's most prominent living female artist."

Frankenthaler is the third daughter of Alfred and Martha Lowenstein Frankenthaler. Although Frankenthaler was raised during the Great Depression, hers was an affluent, privileged upbringing, thanks in part to her father's position as a justice of the New York State Supreme Court. The Frankenthaler children enjoyed numerous cultural advantages, including language and dance lessons, private schooling, and vacations in Maine. Early on, the family recognized Helen's talents and encouraged her interest in art. At the age of nine she won a prize in a children's art contest, and this prize earned her another: her father bought her a gold charm in the shape of an artist's palette. Frankenthaler was very close to her father and was thus devastated when he died of cancer when she was 11 years old. "After he died I was very depressed," she recalled. She remembered feeling "terrible and frightened and alone."

A series of supportive and inspiring teachers helped Frankenthaler through her teens. During her senior year in high school, she was the favorite student of Rufino Tamayo, a well-known Mexican painter. "He showed me how to use my first paint box," Frankenthaler told the *New York Times.* She found other excellent teachers when she attended Bennington College, a progressive school in Vermont. She considered pursuing journalism and criticism, but settled on art while studying with prominent California artist Paul Feeley at Bennington. The style Frankenthaler learned was an abstract (not representational, or intended to represent a specific subject outside the picture) and geometric one, similar to **cubism.**

Forged relationship with critic Clement Greenberg

In 1948, on completing her college degree, Frankenthaler moved back to New York. Not long after, she was asked to organize a show of paintings by Bennington graduates to benefit the college. She invited an array of important figures from the New York art world and was thrilled when noted art critic Clement Greenberg came to the show. "We went around the room together," she told the *New York Times.* "And he finally let me know that he thought my picture was the worst one in the show. At the same time he took my phone number."

This was the beginning of a five-year relationship between Frankenthaler and Greenberg. They painted and traveled together, and he introduced her to the art world of New York. She began socializing with people she had read about in newspapers and magazines, including such prominent artists as Willem and Elaine de Kooning, Franz Kline, and David Smith, who worked in a style called **abstract expressionism.** Their aim was to capture

Helen Frankenthaler

emotion without depicting scenes or subjects, depending instead on powerful colors, large canvases, and almost violent brush strokes. Frankenthaler also began meeting artists her own age who were to become the second generation of abstract expressionists. Included in this group were several women, among them Grace Hartigan and Joan Mitchell. They were some of the first women artists with whom Frankenthaler had contact; her other teachers and colleagues were men. Ultimately, Frankenthaler came to believe that real talent will eventually be recognized, regardless of the artist's gender.

Two of the most important contacts Clement Greenberg provided for Frankenthaler were husband and wife: **Jackson Pollock** (see entry) and Lee Krasner. She and Greenberg spent occasional weekends at Pollock and Krasner's home on Long Island, where Frankenthaler watched the elder artists work. She remembers being astounded and overwhelmed by Pollock's work. Pollock's style was known as "drip" painting. He spread a huge canvas on the floor and dripped and spattered paint from above, moving in a dancelike way around all sides of the canvas. "I was in awe of it, and I wanted to get at why," Frankenthaler recalled.

Developed soak-stain technique

Most of Frankenthaler's colleagues were adherents of Willem de Kooning's more popular technique, which used thick, raucous brush strokes, but she could not get Pollock's drip style out of her mind. One day in 1952, she spread a canvas on the floor of her studio and, rather than dripping paint, poured pigment that had been thinned with turpentine onto her canvas. The result was something totally new. The technique developed because Frankenthaler ignored a rule that all painters learn: that oil paint should not be applied directly to raw canvas fabric. Painters typically employ a substance to "seal" the fabric fibers and prevent the canvas from absorbing the paint. Frankenthaler did not seal her canvas; she poured her paint, which she had thinned to an almost watery liquid, directly onto the raw canvas. The canvas and the colors merged, and the painting became a work made of color rather than of paint lying on a surface. Pollock's technique built up the surface of the canvas using the paint as a key element of texture. Frankenthaler's "soak-stain" technique used color and light on the surface rather than paint itself.

Frankenthaler showed her first stain painting, which she called *Mountains and Sea,* to her friend Greenberg. Recognizing its originality and beauty, he showed the work to two other artists, Morris Louis and Kenneth Noland. They went back to their studios and began working with the stain technique. This was the beginning of the style known as **color field painting.**

In 1989 the editor-in-chief of *American Artist* magazine named Frankenthaler's *Mountains and Sea* one of the four "landmark paintings in the history of contemporary art." This work and others that followed have been praised for their poetic, emotional qualities. Frankenthaler has said she was influenced by watercolor paintings (with which her works are often compared) and the landscape paintings of John Marin and **Paul Cézanne** (see entry).

On her large canvases, Frankenthaler uses sponges, mops, and squeegees to move the paint around. This creates unusual color combinations and flowing, unfolding forms. There is no illusion of space or depth, although the viewer's imagination can sometimes see depth in the way cool colors like blue and green seem to recede and warm colors like red and yellow appear to come forward. Frankenthaler's sharp sense of color—the most important attribute of her work—produces a pure and vibrant light that seems to come from within the painting. Yet the tones of the work would be indefinable without an established sense of space. "Color doesn't work unless it works in space. Color alone is just decoration," she told the *New York Times.* Balancing her undulating "veils" of color in the space of the canvas is crucial to her.

"Think, feel, worry, approach, ACT!"

Frankenthaler does not plan out her paintings and usually begins to paint with no particular idea in mind, though she is often inspired by natural phenomena like clouds, weather, mountains, and the sea. She elaborated her formula to a writer for *Look* magazine, stating, "Think, feel, worry, approach, ACT! Then stand back and look. Edit things out that don't come off." She frequently moves

Flood, 1967. Acrylic on canvas, 124" x 140". Whitney Museum of American Art, New York.

the canvas and herself to get the desired effects. One writer commented, "Each of her paintings has its own weather—serene, turbulent, brooding, but always luminous." After completing a painting, sometimes in just one afternoon, she gives it a title based on the mood it suggests. Many of her titles come from nature, such as *Tulip Tint, Tangerine*, or *Flood*. Others are more descriptive or humorous: *Mother Goose Melody, Fireworks, Summer Banner*. Some, like *Caravan, Pistachio*, and *Into the West*, come from memories of travels around the United States and abroad.

After developing the soak-stain technique, Frankenthaler became a highly successful artist, exhibiting her work frequently throughout the 1950s and 1960s. In 1958 she married the acclaimed abstract expressionist painter Robert Motherwell. During their 13-year marriage they were at the center of the art world in New York. In the 1960s Frankenthaler switched from oil paints to acrylics and experimented with the rectangular shape of the canvas, often adding striped borders. In the late 1960s and early 1970s, she poured overlapping layers of color that suggested sheer drapery or atmospheric conditions, while the late 1970s saw her exploring some of the cubist ideas of space she had learned in art school.

At present, Frankenthaler leads a comfortable life, shuttling between her studio/home in New York City and her country home in Connecticut. She has earned a reputation for elegance and style and enjoys films, traveling, entertaining, and swimming. Frankenthaler is known as a forceful and disciplined person—sometimes even forbidding or stern—but her poetic, creative side is amply evident when she paints.

Certainly other techniques have developed since the color field school was born in the 1950s, but Frankenthaler has not changed her style. In 1989 she told *Newsweek,* "I continue to do the work that I do." Current trends notwithstanding, she has remained faithful to the approach that helped her realize her signature conception of beauty. Indeed, critics have charged that she is overly concerned with beauty, suggesting that her works are too decorative or not "meaningful" enough. But her work continues to be popular and admired for precisely the unadorned emotional effects she has always valued. Rather than copy the styles of her predecessors, Frankenthaler adapted their methods and challenged the rules of painting to develop a new creative process. This has had an enormous impact on contemporary art and guarantees her a vaunted place in its history.

Masterworks

1952	*Mountains and Sea*
1958	*Jacob's Ladder*
1959	*Mother Goose Melody*
1964	*Buddha's Court*
1967	*Flood*
1968	*Summer Banner*
1977	*Caravan*
1982	*Fireworks*
1987	*Scarlatti*

Antonio Gaudi

Born June 25, 1852
Reus, Catalonia, Spain
Died June 10, 1926
Barcelona, Spain

"Gaudi was the greatest architect and (many would say) the greatest cultural figure of any kind that Catalunya had produced since the Middle Ages."

Robert Hughes

The architecture of Antonio Gaudi has been described as "surrealist collage," "well-set jelly," and "dreams in stone." His work did not spawn an imitative school and so, no single phrase has been coined to describe it. His creations—most of them in and around Barcelona, Spain—have become landmarks of that city, drawing thousands of tourists. Indeed, Gaudi's architectural inventions were so far ahead of their time that they have only come to be truly appreciated in the last few decades.

Antonio Gaudi y Cornet was the youngest of five children born to Francisco Gaudi and Antonia Cornet. His mother's male relatives were mostly sailors, while his father descended from a long line of metal workers. From his father, the young Gaudi learned many of the skills of handling metals like copper and wrought iron and cultivated an appreciation for artisanship.

The importance of Gaudi's cultural environment can scarcely be overstated. He was born and lived his entire life in the Spanish province of Catalonia (or Catalunya). The fiercely independent Catalan people, besides speaking a language that is spoken nowhere else in Spain, have struggled to maintain an independant culture in the face of centuries of interference from and occupation by—among others—Romans, Arabs, and the French. This mixture of heritages has helped make Catalonia, and especially its capital city, Barcelona, a flourishing cultural center from the Middle Ages to the present. The ritual and grandeur of Catholicism has also determined the contours of Catalan culture. Gaudi's architecture was a product of this rich confluence.

Gaudi attended religious schools in his hometown and in a larger city nearby. As a child he was fascinated by plants, animals, insects, geology, and weather. The forms and decorations of nature—trees, flowers, mushrooms, vines, bones—later appeared in his designs. Gaudi showed considerable artistic talent as a child; when he reached 18 he traveled to Barcelona to study at its new School of Architecture. Gaudi's grades in the traditional curriculum—architectural history, engineering, and planning—were only fair. It is tempting to believe that his attention wandered because of his unorthodox view of the problems of building and space.

Shunned square corners and flat walls

Architects generally plan a building by drawing maps and pictures of their proposed structure from several points of view, a sensible approach that Gaudi scarcely ever employed. This was in part because he rarely constructed edifices with square corners and flat walls. But it was also due to Gaudi's frequent improvisation, in which he freely added and changed elements as the spirit moved him. In this respect much of his work more closely resembles the inventive spirit of modern painting than modern architecture, which tends to value reason above all.

Although Gaudi was not a brilliant student, his gifts were nonetheless recognized—while still in school he began working on an important park project for the city of Barcelona. One of his professors gave him credit for this project even though he hadn't attended class while working on it. Gaudi spent many hours poring over the school's sizable collection of photographs of "exotic" architecture from North Africa, Persia, India, Egypt, and elsewhere; these photographs stimulated him in his work and inspired, among other developments, his use of glazed tile to decorate buildings. It was fitting that his first commission after graduation was to build a home for a prominent tile manufacturer. Gaudi lavished tile decoration on the Casa Vicens and employed many of the Islamic and other Eastern stylistic touches he had absorbed at school.

A few years after graduation, Gaudi received a commission for construction of a large church in the suburbs of Barcelona. The Church of the Sagrada Familia (Sacred Family) occupied Gaudi for the rest of his life. Its design had been planned by an older architect, and building had begun in 1882. The original architect quit two years later, and the association sponsoring the church's construction chose Gaudi to replace him, giving him a completely free hand in the project. He took the design, which was in the medieval Gothic style, and reworked it to his own liking, creating in the process one of the most unusual churches in the world. Some art historians purport that Gaudi was inspired by mountains in an area of Catalonia where he had worked on restoring a monastery. These mountains are reminiscent of tall, rounded pillars of hardened lava; Gaudi lent this look of melted stone to the towers of Sagrada Familia. Others have compared them to the "drip castles" children make at the beach with wet sand, or to stalagmite formations in a cave. The idea of liquid is carried throughout the structure; "dripping" icicle-like pieces hang from the pointed arches. Carvings of plants and animals and colorful tile **mosaics** cover various surfaces. The entire church—which was never completed—is a powerful monument to the architect's imagination.

Draped iron dragon across Finca Güell gate

Among the most celebrated buildings bearing Gaudi's indelible imprint are two projects he undertook for his friend and patron Eusebi Güell i Bacigalupi, whom he'd met in 1878. Güell—a rising industrialist, politician, and socially important

Church of the Sagrada Familia, Barcelona, 1884–1926. Reproduced by permission of Sipa Press/Art Resource, NY.

| Antonio Gaudi

gentleman in Barcelona—had seen and liked a sculptural display case Gaudi had made. He located the artist and hired him to build projects that would trumpet Güell's wealth and stature in the community. Gaudi designed the main gate of the Finca Güell—his patron's country estate outside of Barcelona—and two nearby buildings. The gate, made of wrought iron, has a huge iron dragon draped across it. Art critic Robert Hughes describes it as "malignantly alive, with every iron tooth and talon, each pleat of its black wing sharp with vitality."

The Palau (Palace) Güell, meanwhile, was the first large building Gaudi designed and built; it displays many of the characteristics that would distinguish his work. Perhaps most important was the skilled artisanship of numerous workers in stone, wood, tile, and wrought iron. Gaudi spared nothing for his friend's large new home, going so far as to design the furniture, window latches, and shutters. In the basement, where the carriage horses were stabled, Gaudi designed the ceiling supports as huge brick "mushrooms," some with round bases and some polygonal. The center of the palace is a tremendous dome capped by a three-story spire. It is decorated in a Moorish, or North African, style with tiles, tinted glass, inlaid wood paneling, and detailed stone carvings.

Another characteristic part of the design is the roof. Unlike most architects, Gaudi did not adhere to the principle that a roof merely covers a structure. Beginning with the Palau Güell and continuing throughout his life's work, he created fantasylands on rooftops. He designed chimneys in whimsical shapes and covered them with a crazy-quilt pattern of colored tile and glass mosaic. This tile work, called *trencadis,* traditionally employs scraps of tile and glass. But Gaudi was ahead of his time in recycling materials; he encouraged his workers to gather glass bottles, tiles, and ceramic plates they found in the streets for use in the mosaics. Gaudi fancied the fragmented design of the *trencadis,* particularly the way its appearance was altered as the light reflected on it changed, sometimes even seeming to dissolve. It is possible that these broken, geometric designs influenced **Pablo Picasso** (see entry) in his development of **cubism.** Picasso lived near the Palau Güell during his student years in Barcelona.

Gaudi began two other projects for Eusebi Güell. The Colonia Güell was a planned neighborhood for Güell's textile workers on the outskirts of Barcelona. Gaudi designed and built the church, which was never finished due to Güell's death in 1918. The crypt, or underground chapel portion, of the structure, however, was completed.

Attained structural perfection with crypt

Gaudi designed the space by using a model made of strings and weights. He drew the ground plan and then hung a string from each point where a column would support the structure. He joined these strings with cross strings and weights to determine the areas where structural pressure or tension would be greatest. He then photographed the string model and turned the photographs upside down to reverse the whole structure. No one had ever designed a building in this manner, though such methods would become common once computer imaging came into use some 75 years later. In fact, when modern architects approximated Gaudi's design by computer, they found that it was structurally perfect—as if he'd had access to such modern contrivances.

The crypt design has been called a masterwork, "one of the greatest architectural spaces in Europe." The support columns lean like huge, ancient tree trunks, lending the burial ground a mysterious and theatrical air. The massive vaulted ceiling and angled walls make the space seem to expand and contract like a breathing body. Indeed, wrote Hughes, the visitor feels "like Jonah in the belly of the brick whale."

The Güell Park was originally planned as a housing project, but it never progressed beyond open spaces and the great plaza. It has become a favorite spot for the people of Barcelona to play, jog, and stroll. Gaudi designed the two entrance pavilions in his typical curving style. They are covered in *trencadis* mosaic and have been compared to the gingerbread houses imagined in Grimm's fairy tales. The area also features fountains, sculptures, snaky benches, and a "Greek" temple. In the rock garden, viewers feel that they are walking through a dreamlike landscape similar to those conjured by the **surrealists**—an amusement park born of Gaudi's fertile imagination. This garden was a great influence on another Catalan artist, the surrealist **Salvador Dali** (see entry).

Two residential buildings that Gaudi designed have also survived as masterpieces of his style. The Casa Batlló was a renovation of an apartment building. The Casa Milá was a new structure, described as "a sea cliff with caves in it for people." The wavy lines of the exteriors of these buildings, as well as the fanciful chimneys and ventilators on their roofs have made them world-renowned landmarks. The chimney tops and stairway exits recall ancient Greek helmets, with huge dark openings for eyes. Some say they resemble futuristic centurion helmets not unlike those featured in the *Star Wars* film series.

Concocted underground garage

In the Casa Milá, Gaudi wanted to use a double ramp winding up and down the light well of the structure so that residents could drive their cars right to the doors of their apartments. (This was in 1905 when few people actually had cars.) Ultimately, the auto ramp would have required too much space, so Gaudi had to settle for a pedestrian ramp. He did, however, install an underground parking lot, the first ever built in Barcelona.

After completing the Casa Milá in about 1910, Gaudi worked on little besides the Sagrada Familia church. He became something of a recluse, living by himself in a small house in the Park Güell and overseeing the church construction. He was celebrated as a legendary and mysterious figure, but few really understood his architecture. When he was hit and killed by a trolley in 1926, police could not initially identify the strange old man in the rumpled black suit. But a few days later, more than ten thousand mourners followed his casket to the chapel of Sagrada Familia, where he was buried. Debate continued as to whether his work was simply outrageous or amazingly creative

Casa Milá, Barcelona, 1905–10. Reproduced by permission ▶ of Giraudon/Art Resource, NY.

Masterworks

1878-90	Casa Vicens
1884-1926	Church of the Sagrada Familia
1885-89	Palau Güell
1900-14	Park Güell
1905-07	Casa Batlló
1905-10	Casa Milá

and exciting. Architects have come to appreciate that behind and underneath the curving, winding, and colorful forms are the calculations of a genius who understood advanced concepts of engineering and was skilled in utilizing a variety of materials in previously unheard of ways.

Admiration of and controversy over Gaudi's work has endured. When the 1992 Olympic Games were held in Barcelona, interest in his unique architecture was renewed. The Olympic mascot was depicted on posters carrying the Sagrada Familia Church under its arm as a symbol of the city. Contention continues to this day over whether the church should be finished; while one group of architects and artists works to complete the structure, others circulate petitions and picket various sites to stop the work and leave the church as Gaudi left it. Whether this work is ultimately finished or not, Gaudi's influence on modern architecture remains. As a Catalan professor of architecture told *Time* magazine in 1991, "We're still learning from Gaudi's genius."

Paul Gauguin

Born June 7, 1848
Paris, France
Died May 8, 1903
Atuana Hiva-Oa, Marquesas Islands

In the early 1880s Paul Gauguin was living a very traditional life as a Parisian stockbroker, family man, and weekend painter. He particularly enjoyed painting and began to meet other painters in Paris and even show some of his works in exhibits. By 1883 the desire to become an artist had turned his life upside down and would ultimately lead him to Denmark, Brittany, Martinique, and finally to the islands of the South Pacific. The tales of poverty and misery that have developed around Gauguin's life have made him a romantic symbol of the struggling artist. His artworks have been studied and admired for their poetic sense, vivid colors, and "suggestive magic."

Eugène Henri-Paul Gauguin's life of travel and adventure began at an early age. His mother, Aline Chazal, was half-Peruvian and the daughter of a socialist political leader. His father, Clovis Gauguin, was a journalist. Political events in 1851 caused the family to leave France and sail to Peru to join family there. Gauguin was only three years old when his father died during the voyage

"I am not a painter who works from nature. With me, everything happens in my wild imagination."

▲ *Portrait:* Self-portrait
Reproduced by permission of The Bettman Archive.

to Peru. His mother continued the journey with Paul and his sister. They spent four years living in a big house in the capital city, Lima, with their uncle and his family. Some of the exotic things young Gauguin saw and experienced remained in his memory: tropical birds and flowers, elaborately decorated buildings, moonlit tropical nights, and even an earthquake.

When the Gauguin family returned to France, Paul was seven and spoke only Spanish. They went to live with their grandfather in Orléans, a city in central France. When Gauguin started school that year he had a lot of trouble because his French was so poor. But he soon learned the language and became a good student.

Began as stockbroker and family man

At 17, Gauguin signed on as a pilot's assistant in the merchant marine in order to fulfill his required military service. After three years, he joined the navy, spending two more years there. His travels gave him the chance to see many new and different parts of the world. In 1871 Gauguin returned to Paris and secured a position as a stockbroker, at which he was very successful. In 1873 he married a Danish woman, Mette Sophie Gad. They settled into a comfortable life and over the next ten years had five children.

Gauguin had always been interested in art. He began painting on the weekends as a hobby. He also visited galleries and started buying paintings by some of the newest painters of the day, including **Paul Cézanne, Claude Monet, Pierre-Auguste Renoir** (see entries), and others working in the style of **impressionism.** Gauguin was even able to meet some of his favorite artists through his growing friendship with artist Camille Pissarro. As he spent more time painting, he rented a studio and showed paintings in the impressionist exhibitions held in 1881 and 1882. He spent two summer vacations painting in the country with Pissarro, and he met Cézanne, who also painted with Pissarro occasionally.

The progress Gauguin made in his painting encouraged his growing desire to give up his job as a stockbroker and devote himself to art. Finally, in January 1883, without warning his family, Gauguin quit his job. Most of his friends thought he was crazy to give up a secure career and well-established household. Nonetheless, Gauguin moved his family to Rouen, a city northwest of Paris. He believed they could live more cheaply there and that he could support them by selling his paintings. Eight months later they were almost penniless and were thus forced to move to Denmark to live with his wife's family.

Circumstances worsened as Gauguin became increasingly despondent. His Danish relatives could understand neither him nor his paintings. He left Denmark and returned to Paris with one of his young sons. But life there was no better as Gauguin still had little money; both father and son became seriously ill. Despite this, Gauguin managed to paint and exhibit several pictures that were received favorably by critics. Once again, Gauguin decided to leave the expensive city of Paris, this time headed for Brittany, an agricultural province in the northwest of France. The town of Pont-Aven became Gauguin's home for the next four or five years, trips to Paris, Panama, and Martinique notwithstanding.

Developed synthetism

It was in Pont-Aven that he began to develop the style for which he is best known, synthetism. For Gauguin, synthetism was a reaction to the way impressionist painters used color and light in an attempt to capture how things looked in nature. Conversely, he longed to use the elements of nature only as they fit the mood or emotion of the scene he wished to paint. The main elements of synthetism are the use of dark outlines, strong colors, flat forms, and few shadows.

In trying to develop this new style and still looking for an affordable place to live, Gauguin sold all of his belongings in 1887 and left France for Panama, where he hoped to get a job with his brother-in-law. He lasted only one month as a laborer on the Panama Canal before departing for the island of Martinique in the West Indies. Gauguin loved the wild colors and variations of the landscape there, the volcanic mountains and valleys full of flowers. But he was still unable to earn a

living and so returned to Paris. This sojourn in Martinique confirmed in Gauguin his desire to escape the false values and greed of European society and to live in a less sophisticated world. He admired what he called the "primitive" nature of the inhabitants and found that his artistic impulses responded well to the people and their surroundings. For the next few years he made plans to "leave society."

During this period and for the rest of his life Gauguin struggled with two key problems: his constant lack of funds and loneliness. He missed his family in Denmark but had little inclination to join them there. He sold few paintings and suffered hunger and illness. Then, during one of his many stays in Paris, Gauguin met the Dutch painter **Vincent van Gogh** (see entry) in an artists' supply shop. The two saw each other frequently and in 1888, when van Gogh moved to the south of France, he invited Gauguin to join him. Gauguin followed his colleague in the fall of that year. For two months the relationship between the two artists deteriorated; their temperaments were very different and they had few ideas in common about art. By December they had had a terrible fight and Gauguin had departed, first returning to Paris and then to Pont-Aven. It was shortly after this calamitous event that van Gogh, in great emotional distress, cut off part of his ear.

Prefigured work of Picasso and Matisse

Over the course of the next two years Gauguin produced some of his most famous paintings. Two especially are prized for their creativity and modern sensibility. In one, *Still Life with Three Puppies,* Gauguin demonstrates several progressive artistic concepts; he does away with the illusion of space or **perspective,** employing instead large areas of flat color and pattern to create space and depth. It would be another decade or two before artists like **Henri Matisse** and **Pablo Picasso** (see entries) would build on these ideas. Indeed, Gauguin is considered by many to be a crucial link in the progression of contemporary art from **impressionism** to **cubism** and beyond.

The other standout work from this period is *The Vision after the Sermon (Jacob Wrestling the Angel).* It depicts a group of women from Brittany, adorned by their traditional white headdresses, witnessing a vision of the biblical Jacob wrestling with the Angel of Death. The painting is divided by a strong diagonal across the center. The women are shown at the left, very close to the picture's surface. Viewers feel that they are standing in the midst of the crowd. The angel and Jacob are in the upper right corner and seem very far away. They are painted against a bright red background. Gauguin utilizes many of the same methods in this painting as he had in *Three Puppies,* but with an intensely spiritual result. The scene comes directly from Gauguin's imagination. He felt no need to portray color, form, or space as they would appear in nature. This was an important departure from previous conventions of painting.

By this time Gauguin knew that he needed a complete break with society and "civilization" in order to pursue his artistic vision. Longing to devote himself completely to his art and not to the pursuit of income, he sold all of his paintings at auction and sailed for Tahiti in the spring of 1890, sure that there he would find the luxurious tropical paradise about which he dreamed. He was disappointed at first because the port at which he landed, Papeete, appeared quite European. But Gauguin soon obtained a piece of land in the interior of the island and built a native-style house.

He lived and painted there for two years, until his money ran out and he was forced to return to Paris once again. His paintings from these years do not differ greatly in style from his Pont-Aven works, but the subjects portrayed—the landscape, animals, and people of Tahiti—and rich colors amply reflect his new environment. Gauguin became more and more convinced that painting should be a very personal expression of the artist. He believed it was imperative that artists feel free to change, distort, and exaggerate what they saw in order to express their artistic vision. These convictions are clear in the works *We Greet Thee, Mary (Ia Orana Maria)* and *In the Market (Ta Matete)*.

Returned to South Pacific

When Gauguin was forced to return to Paris in 1893 for financial reasons, he was determined to spend as little time there as possible. For once, luck was with him; he received a small inheritance from an uncle who had died recently. But the painter immediately spent most of the money on an extravagant apartment and new clothes. He held another auction of his paintings, selling only 11 of 43. He sold whatever other possessions he could and returned to the South Pacific, this time for good.

Though he lived in poverty and was often ill and alone, paintings from his last years show great beauty, sensuality, and emotion. By then Gauguin had been influenced by the artistic styles of many cultures, including those of Egypt, Persia, Italy, and Japan. Perhaps the most celebrated work of this later period is *Where Do We Come From? What Are We? Where Are We Go-*

ing? It is richly decorated and depicts the source of life, scenes from everyday life, and death beyond life. Gauguin considered it his masterwork. "I believe it's ... my best canvas," he wrote. "I have put into it, before dying, all of my energy, such a grieving passion amid terrible circumstances and a vision so complete ... life surges into it."

In 1898, after painting *Where Do We Come From?*, Gauguin attempted suicide but failed. After recovering, he lived for several years, though often suffering from illness. A friend in Paris made his last years a bit easier by selling his paintings and forwarding the proceeds. Collectors and other artists slowly began to appreciate the value of his art, but this financial and artistic success came too late. Nonetheless, his bold, innovative style and commitment to personal expression, as well as the dogged pursuit of his muse despite enormous sacrifice make Gauguin one of the greatest and most influential of what are now considered modern artists.

Masterworks

1888	*Still Life with Three Puppies*
	Vision after the Sermon (Jacob Wrestling the Angel)
1891	*Tahitian Landscape*
	We Greet Thee, Mary (Ia Orana Maria)
1892	*In the Market (Ta Matete)*
1894	*Day of the God (Mahana No Atua)*
1897	*Where Do We Come From? What Are We? Where Are We Going?*
1899	*Tahitian Women with Mango Blossoms*

Vincent van Gogh

Born March 30, 1853
Groot Zundert, Holland
Died July 29, 1890
Auvers-sur-Oise, France

"What I'm trying to do is not to faithfully imitate on canvas what I see before me but rather to use color in the most arbitrary way to express myself better."

Vincent van Gogh's troubled life and tragic death have fascinated people since he committed suicide over 100 years ago. The paintings and drawings he left have appreciated considerably in that time and are now among the most valuable and popular in the world. The unmistakable intensity of his work—his color sense, use of pigments, and above all, his emotional expression—has influenced many of the greatest artists of the twentieth century. And the indelible images he created, including numerous self-portraits, raucous sunflowers, and the swirling blues of the night sky, are some of the most copied in history.

Vincent Willem van Gogh was raised in a small town in Holland where his father, the Reverend Theodorus van Gogh, was the pastor of the town's Calvinist church. Van Gogh's mother, Anna Cornelia Carbentus, was a woman of formidable character who busied herself with local charity work and shouldered the lion's share of responsibility for bringing up her six children, of whom Vincent was the oldest. Beginning in early childhood, van Gogh struggled with the demands of society. He was unusually shy and spent a lot of time by himself. He also had a very quick temper and sometimes became violent. Yet he loved to wander in the countryside collecting flowers and insects, observing the colors of the sunset or watching the wind move the leaves. The only person close to van Gogh was his younger brother Theo, who was able to draw him out and get him to talk about his problems. Throughout their lives, Theo consistently supported his brother emotionally and financially. We know much about the artist's life from the many letters exchanged by the two over the years.

Mother encourages troubled child to draw

Van Gogh's school years were not particularly notable. He was uninterested and often unruly, but he did spend time reading the many books in his father's library and seemed truly inspired by his father's Sunday sermons. His parents were at a loss to handle this child, though his mother was sympathetic and encouraged the boy in his early attempts to express himself through drawing.

When van Gogh was 16, his father arranged for him to work in an art gallery with his uncle in The Hague. The family hoped that his interest in art would lead him to a successful career in the gallery world. He did well at first and enjoyed being around the sculptures and paintings that came through the gallery. After a few years van Gogh was sent to work in a branch office in London. There he was able to visit several world-renowned museums and view works by British artists. But his happiness in London did not last long. He fell in love with a young woman who rejected him; the artist was deeply wounded and returned to his sullen, often volatile behavior.

Still seeking answers to the questions about himself that had plagued him as a boy, van Gogh turned to religion. He became fervently involved in religious ideas and missionary work over the next few years. By the time he was 25, he was working as a missionary in the coal-mining region of Belgium. He had given away most of his belongings and lived in a shack. But his

◀ *Portrait (p. 144):* Self-portrait. *Reproduced by permission of Archive Photos/Camera Press.*

fanaticism, manifested by an overzealous devotion to his work, actually led to his termination by the missionary organization for which he worked.

Captures misery of coal miners

All along he continued to draw. His work from this period features miners and peasants living in the most dire of circumstances, in dingy huts with little food. He drew groups of women staggering under huge loads of coal on their backs. His most famous work inspired by this time—though it was painted several years after he left the area—is the *Potato Eaters*. The family of peasants gathered around the table in their dark hovel have only a plate of potatoes to share. Their weathered hands indicate hard labor, their faces fatigue and despair. The colors in the painting, mostly black, brown, and gray, are typical of van Gogh's work in these days. The artist shows us with great sympathy the wretched condition of the people he was trying to help and his own sadness as well. "Life has the color of dishwater," he wrote to Theo. Still, despite his uncertainties, van Gogh was increasingly convinced that he was destined to become an artist.

The next few years found van Gogh wandering both physically and psychologically. He lived for a time in Brussels, Belgium, and in The Hague, where he studied with several artists. He also resided with his parents on several occasions, but these episodes always ended with him leaving in anger. In a pattern that would plague him throughout his life, he forged weak relationships with women that ended badly. Spells of depression and illness, a regular occurrence when he lived in cold apartments with little to eat, were common in these years, relieved only by van Gogh's work. Theo faithfully wrote to him from Paris, where he was working in a gallery, sending money and words of encouragement.

In the fall of 1885, van Gogh moved to Antwerp, Belgium. He seemed to be functioning more fully, socializing with other

◄ Sunflowers. *The National Gallery, London.*

painters and visiting galleries and museums. He was especially fascinated by the works of Flemish painter **Peter Paul Rubens** (see entry). The active figures, unrestrained emotion, and rich colors bewitched van Gogh, who began to use some of these elements in his work. At the port of Antwerp, he came across woodblock prints from Japan and China, which caught his eye for their brightness and flat, clear colors.

Exchanges ideas with impressionists in Paris

In the winter of 1886, van Gogh once again became ill. After several weeks of recovery, he decided to join Theo in Paris. The reunited brothers shared an apartment. Van Gogh's two years in Paris were very stimulating. Theo introduced him to the young, struggling artists of the day, including **Claude Monet, Pierre-Auguste Renoir, Henri Toulouse-Lautrec, Georges Seurat** (see entries), Edgar Degas, and Camille Pissarro. Van Gogh spent many hours at Paris cafés with these painters, most of whom would come to be called **impressionists,** discussing the newest notions concerning color, light, and nature. The effects on van Gogh's work were immediate; his colors became lighter and more vivid and his subjects less disturbed.

During his second winter in Paris, van Gogh met **Paul Gauguin** (see entry), another painter who was searching for purpose and expression in his art. They became friends, and van Gogh was able to exhibit some of his paintings in a shop owned by Gauguin's father. But he did not sell anything. In fact, he had never sold a single piece.

While in Paris van Gogh began using himself as a model more frequently; over 15 self-portraits from a three-year period, 1887-90, have survived. Other artists, among them the German **Albrecht Dürer** and van Gogh's countryman **Rembrandt van Rijn** (see entries), left us series of self-portraits, so we can see their stylistic development as well as the process of aging. But van Gogh's self-portraits are different; there is little movement in time but an incredible range of emotions and psychological states. In those three years, we see van Gogh as a dapper gentleman of Paris, a rail-thin, ghostly painter clutching his palette and brushes,

a seemingly cruel, sunken-cheeked creature, and a doomed and pathetic figure, the space encircling him filled with tense and disorienting swirls. What ties the self-portraits together is the ability of the artist to illustrate the force of his experiences through his use of color, distortion of form, and control of brush strokes. These are the techniques that would lead art critics to label van Gogh's style **expressionism.**

Renewed by sunshine of Arles

By the winter of 1888, van Gogh's mental condition had begun to deteriorate; perhaps the gloomy weather and lack of financial success were too much. The painter also began to feel

The Starry Night, 1889.
Oil on canvas, 29"x 36¼".
The Museum of Modern Art,
New York. Acquired through
the Lillie P. Bliss Bequest.
Photograph © 1995 The
Museum of Modern Art,
New York.

that he was becoming a burden on his brother. One day he packed his case, left a note for Theo, and took the train to Arles, a town in the south of France near the Mediterranean Sea. The impact of the warm, sunny climate and beautiful surroundings was enormous. Van Gogh began painting with remarkable vigor. With his brush, he captured orchards, riverbanks, bridges, flowers, haystacks, wheat fields, and sailboats, and with each painting his colors got lighter and brighter until he was using pure color right out of the paint tubes, often applying it in thick splotches. This creative energy, much of it expelled in extreme heat and heavy exposure to sunlight, eventually exhausted him. At the same time, van Gogh seemed to become obsessed with the color yellow; for several weeks he painted nothing but sunflowers. These would one day become some of his most beloved work.

His letters to and from Theo brought van Gogh into close contact with the local postman, who, along with his family, befriended the painter and often served as his model. Arguably his most famous portraits from this period are *Postman Roulin* and *La Berceuse,* a painting of the postman's wife. Also from this time emerged scenes of the local café and of van Gogh's room. In the fall of 1888, Gauguin came to Arles to live with van Gogh and for a while, the two supported each other and lived together peacefully. Van Gogh hoped other artists from Paris would join them and start an artists' community in Arles. But Gauguin did not find Arles as inspiring as had his colleague, nor did he find it easy to live in such close proximity to van Gogh's frenzied working style. Increasingly violent quarrels ensued until finally, Gauguin announced in December 1888 that he was leaving. This abandonment was beyond van Gogh's fragile coping skills; he suffered a severe mental breakdown during which he cut off part of his earlobe. When he recovered enough to leave the hospital, he painted two self-portraits showing his bandaged head underneath a fur cap.

Months after his break with Gauguin, van Gogh entered an asylum, where he hoped to find some peace. He was able to paint there, but the wild brush strokes and severe irregularity of the forms depicted in these works suggest that peace was nowhere to be found. The artist did regain some stability by the fall of 1889, but he worried constantly about his future and his continuing dependence on Theo.

Sells a painting—the only one

In early 1890 van Gogh was given a boost by the news that Theo had sold one of his paintings. It was the first and only painting sold during his lifetime. This led to such now-prized works as *Cornfield with Reaper* and *The Starry Night,* which illuminates the sparkling, spiraling starlight over Arles. Still, the twisted, rigid shapes of these efforts hint that van Gogh was not past his mental infirmities.

By the spring of 1890, van Gogh felt the need to return to Paris to be near Theo, who set him up in a room in a small town near Paris under the care of a specialist. The doctor was also an art lover and encouraged van Gogh to continue painting, even sitting as a model for him. Van Gogh attacked his canvases as a man possessed in these spring months, producing over 60 paintings, among them *Wheatfield with Crows.* But black days began to bury the artist, and soon a severe depression overcame him. On July 27, 1890, he shot himself in the abdomen. He survived for two days, Theo ever by his side.

Like many artists before him, van Gogh was keenly intent on uncovering the beauty of nature and the extent of his feelings. What sets him apart from the artists who preceded him and also links him to modern artists, was his ability to do away with "accuracy" of shape and color in order to graphically express his emotions. The colors he employed, while perhaps not "realistic," depicted the life of his subjects; his bold brush strokes gave motion to trees, stars, flowers, and the very air. And although viewers of his time found his paintings crude and even frightening, contemporary observers have come to understand and fully appreciate van Gogh's unique and enduring artistic vision.

Masterworks	
1880	*Bearers of the Burden*
1885	*Potato Eaters*
1887	*Père Tanguy*
1888	*Orchard*
	Sailing Boats at Les Saintes Maries
	Postman Roulin
	Sunflowers
	The Night Café
	The Arlesienne
1889	*The Starry Night*
1890	*Portrait of Dr. Gachet*
	Wheatfield with Crows

Francisco Goya

*Born March 30, 1746
Fuendetodos, Spain
Died April 16, 1828
Bordeaux, France*

*"I have had
three teachers,
Velazquez,
Rembrandt,
and Nature."*

In eighteenth-century Spain, masters of painting came almost universally from other countries; customarily, the king invited foreign artists, mostly Italians, to paint for him. At the end of the century, however, Francisco Goya emerged as the greatest Spanish painter since **Diego Velazquez** (see entry). The most popular portrait painter of the day, Goya, like Velazquez, was appointed court painter. But despite his position at the foot of power, Goya's posterity derives from works often considered uncharacteristic of someone in such a position: etchings that attacked intolerance, superstition, frivolity, and the evils of war. Because of his enormous influence on nineteenth-century artists such as Eugene Delacroix and **Edouard Manet** (see entry), he is sometimes called the father of modern painting.

Francisco José de Goya y Lucientes was born in a small town in Spain to José Goya, a craftsman, and Gracia Lucientes. His family moved to the nearby town of Saragossa, and Francisco was enrolled in art school, where he became acquainted with the three Bayeu brothers, whose sister, Josefa, he married in 1775. Volumes of stories have circulated about Goya's escapades during his teenage years, including street fights, knifings, and even escape from a death sentence at an Italian prison. Historians have had difficulty separating truth from myth in their studies of the artist's youth, but these anecdotes certainly serve to enhance Goya's legendary status.

Establishes reputation as tapestry painter

It has been firmly established, however, that Goya spent time in Rome during these years, where he no doubt saw and was influenced by the great works of the **Renaissance;** when he returned to Spain, he immersed himself in religious painting and church decoration. In 1776 his brother-in-law, Francisco Bayeu, secured for him a position in the royal tapestry factory in Madrid, Spain's capital city. During the next 17 years he created designs (called cartoons) for countless tapestries, most of them depicting scenes of everyday Spanish life. His delicate brushwork, reliance on vivid color, and expert use of light and shadow made these works tremendously coveted.

In 1780 Goya began painting portraits at the royal court; not long after, he was appointed official court painter. By the age of 40 he was the most popular painter in Madrid. His reputation stemmed from his remarkably discerning eye; though his portraits were often unflattering to their subjects, they seemed to express an undeniable truth. In fact, Goya's 1800 group portrait of the royal family depicted the king as fat and pompous and the queen as shallow and bad-tempered. In this famous painting, *The Family of Charles IV,* Goya makes reference to his predecessor Velazquez and his painting *Las Meninas*. Like the older master, Goya presented the royal family in his studio and painted himself in the background at his easel; it has been alleged that he posed the queen in the same manner as the little princess in *Las Meninas.*

By the late 1780s the tone of Goya's tapestry cartoons and other drawings had become more serious. The events leading up to the 1789 revolution in France affected Goya and other

egalitarian-minded Spaniards very deeply; they hoped that the democratic and liberal ideas that were overtaking the old French order would bring about similar changes in Spain. During the 1790s the Spanish political climate seemed to swing pendulum-like from liberal to reactionary.

Arrested for antigovernment painting

It was during one of the more liberal periods that Goya published a series of **etchings** (drawings on metal plates that can be printed) called *Los Caprichos* (*The Caprices* or *Fancies*). This is the first of four series Goya completed during his lifetime; the *Caprichos* heap scorn on the government and society at large for such evils as greed, laziness, corruption, and cruelty. These powerfully imaginative drawings represent the extreme, righteously indignant side of Goya's prodigious creativity: they conjure a world of witches, monsters, starving skeletons, and fantastic birds. These unreal and often terrifying figures symbolized a variety of injustices and were a far cry from the artist's formal, traditional court paintings. Shortly after the publication of these drawings, Goya was arrested for antigovernment activity. He was eventually released, but the actions of the authorities only underlined the power of his work.

Another powerful influence on Goya during these years was the deafness he suffered due to an illness in 1792. Because he could not hear, he was cut off from most social events, a circumstance that may well have embittered him. Yet his reliance on his other senses may also have improved his already celebrated powers of observation.

In the early years of the nineteenth century, Napoleon I rose to power in France and began conquering large portions of Europe to establish an empire. His armies encountered little resistance when they entered Spain, and in 1808 his brother, Joseph Bonaparte, became King of Spain. The Spanish people hoped that political change would follow, but they were gravely disappointed. On Sunday May 2, 1808, the citizens of Madrid revolted against the invaders. They fought the well-armed French soldiers with only knives, clubs, and stones. That night the soldiers prowled the streets, rooting out the leaders of the revolt and shooting them.

Tres de Mayo's infamous firing squad

Goya's apartment was located in the middle of the area in which these events transpired, and he may have witnessed much of the fighting and the executions; he expressed his outrage on canvas. *Dos de Mayo (The Second of May)* and *Tres de Mayo (The Third of May)* are among the most powerful historical paintings ever created. *Tres de Mayo* portrays a firing squad, seen as anonymous figures from the back, aiming at a group of men

Tres de Mayo (The Third of May), 1808, *1814. Oil on canvas, approx. 8'8" x 11'13". Museo del Prado, Madrid. Reproduced by permission of Alinari/Art Resource, NY.*

whose faces are contorted in fear and horror. Goya draws the viewer's attention to the central victim by focusing light on his bright white shirt. The only other prominent color in this painting full of grays, browns, and blacks is the red of the blood already saturating the ground.

After the defeat of Napoleon, the Spanish king was restored to the throne, and all liberal or democratic ideas were crushed. By this time Goya was an old man; he lived in his country house, known as the *Quinta del Sordo (House of the Deaf Man)*. He covered its walls with **frescoes** of dark and disturbing images and grotesque figures. It was also during this period that he created another series of etchings, *Los Desastres de la Guerra (The Horrors of War)*. These expressive and nightmarish visions have inspired comparisons to the key works of modern **surrealism.**

In 1815 Goya found himself in trouble with the government again. He was investigated for a painting called *The Naked Maja*. It was unusual in Spanish art to paint female nudes due to the imperatives of the conservative government and the Catholic Church. Goya's controversial painting depicts a *maja*, a young courtesan/entertainer similar to the geishas of Japan. She is comfortably lounging on a beautifully decorated couch. The work was shocking at the time, just as Manet's painting *Olympia*—which pays homage to Goya's *Maja*—shocked the public 50 years later. Goya was acquitted of the accusations involving this painting, but his disdain for the government intensified.

When he was 78 years old and completely disillusioned with the politics and society of Spain, Goya petitioned the king to let him leave the country and move to France. He settled in Bordeaux, in the southwest of his newly adopted country, and began to work on a series of **lithographs** of bullfight scenes. Drawing with a special crayon on stone, he was able to work more freely and quickly than in his etchings. These final drawings and his last paintings are distinguished by a marked air of liberation. Away from the strictures of his native country, perhaps Goya felt that he could set aside political and social commentary and paint what brought him pleasure. Unfortunately, he enjoyed only four years in Bordeaux before his death in 1828.

As an artist Goya occupied two different worlds at once; he was able to delight the royal court with portraits in the traditional style that still managed to be slyly rebellious. In his personal work, he confronted tyranny with a powerful eloquence and sharp wit. Countless artists who have used visual means to counter injustice have acknowledged Goya's pioneering importance. In his style and the content of his works, he has exercised a profound influence on most of the major painters of the nineteenth and twentieth centuries.

Masterworks

1793	*The Madhouse at Saragossa*
1798	*Portrait of Ferdinand Guillemardet*
	The Naked Maja
1799	*Los Caprichos* (etchings)
1800	*The Family of Charles IV*
1808-20	*Los Desastres de la Guerra*
1814	*Dos de Mayo (Second of May)*
	Tres de Mayo (Third of May)
1826-27	*The Bordeaux Milkmaid*

El Greco

Born in 1541
Candia, Crete
Died April 1614
Toledo, Spain

El Greco was a modern painter long before what is commonly known as the modern era.

▲ *Portrait:* Self-portrait. *c.1610-12. The Metropolitan Museum of Art, New York. Reproduced by permission of The Bettmann Archive.*

El Greco's mystical, emotional religious paintings and probing portraits were not well understood in his day; in fact, it took nearly three centuries for his work to be appreciated. After mastering the conventions of the Italian **Renaissance** style of his time, he broke with them to express his dramatic visions. In this respect he was a modern painter long before what is commonly known as the modern era.

Domenikos Theotokopoulos was born on the island of Crete, a part of Greece. He spent most of his adult life in Italy and Spain, where he was called El Greco, the Greek. Not much is known about his life in Crete, but as an artist he was most likely educated in the Byzantine style of the eastern Mediterranean. Byzantine art was mostly religious in theme; existing **mosaics** in this style are considered among the most beautiful in the world. Crete was under the rule of Venice, Italy, for many centuries, including the span of El Greco's life. Like many art-

The Resurrection of Christ.
*Museo del Prado, Madrid.
Reproduced by permission
of Alinari/Art Resource, NY.*

About Byzantine Art

Byzantine art is prized for its glittering gold mosaics—pictures made from tiny pieces of tile and glass fitted together like a jigsaw puzzle. Mosaics from Byzantine times most often depicted the monumental figures of Christianity, dressed in richly patterned fabrics. The primary purpose of these representations was less to portray reality than to inspire awe and faith.

In around 311 the Roman emperor Constantine declared the Christian Church to be the official church of the Roman Empire. About a dozen years later, he moved the capital of the empire to the city of Byzantium in what is now Turkey. The city was renamed Constantinople in his honor and soon became among the most important cities in the world. Thus the school of church-oriented art that developed around the imperial court came to be known as Byzantine art.

Greek and Roman artists in pre-Christian times focused on the beauty of the human form and strove to create the illusion of depth in their art. They produced statues of gods and goddesses, which became objects of religious devotion. In trying to spread the new Christian faith, church officials established careful guidelines for the decoration of churches to differentiate Christian embellishment from that of earlier faiths. They banned statuary, adhering to the biblical prohibition of "graven images." Fortunately, these church fathers deemed painting and other pictorial art useful for educating the masses about Christianity. Artists of this time were experts in mosaic, which generally employed small glass squares to compose a picture. The mosaics they produced for Byzantine

ists of his time, the young man traveled to Venice when he was about 25 to study with the masters of Venetian painting, notably **Titian** (see entry) and Tintoretto.

It is believed that El Greco spent three or four years in Venice, where he quickly learned the techniques and ideas of the Venetian Renaissance style. His talents were recognized in short order. He departed for Rome in 1570 when an artist friend obtained a position for him painting for a wealthy family. El Greco soon mastered the techniques pioneered by **Leonardo da Vinci, Michelangelo** (see entries), and the other masters, including **perspective,** sfumato (softening the outline of a form by blending its colors with those of its surroundings) and the use of rich color.

churches remain among the most celebrated in the world.

Because their primary mission was to illustrate sacred figures and events, Byzantine artists developed a style that often seems stiff and simplistic to the modern eye. They were not trying to imitate nature, but to illustrate holy bodies in the eternal space of heaven. As the tradition developed, certain characteristics emerged. For one, the tall, thin figures in mosaic depiction are usually seen from the front. The beautifully decorative draperies adorning the figures provided the artists ample opportunity to display their skills; various tones of rich color in the glass approximate the patterns and curves of the cloth. Uniformly flat, gold backgrounds suggest to viewers that the subjects portrayed do not inhabit an earthly space and lend a wonderful splendor to the church interior. The simplicity of the style allows nothing to distract from the purpose of educating and inspiring faith.

The Byzantine style was dominant from about the fourth century until well past the year 1000. It influenced art throughout Europe, the Middle East, and Russia. While European art gradually evolved into the style we call medieval, the elements of Byzantine art played an important role in Greek and Russian art well into the nineteenth century. Examples of this form remain on the walls of churches in Italy, Greece, and Turkey. Much of the impact of these works is dependent on viewing them in their proper setting, the lights and shadows of the church contributing to the spiritual experience. Few photographs, divorced from this context, can fully capture the awesome power of the Byzantine masters.

Settles in Toledo, Spain

He took these skills with him to Spain in 1577. It is possible that he traveled there on the advice of Spanish friends in Rome in the hope of finding work at the new palace-museum-church called the Escorial then being constructed by King Philip II. El Greco and his companion, Jeronima de las Cuevas, settled in Toledo, just north of the capital city of Madrid; their son, Jorge Manuel, was born in 1578. He later became a painter.

The tremendous wealth, power, and influence of the Church meant that religious art was in great demand; El Greco found work immediately. One of his first paintings was for the Cathedral of Toledo. Entitled *El Espolio* or *The Disrobing of Christ,* it was El Greco's largest work up to that time and bears elements of the styles he had learned in Crete and Italy. It also displays early attributes of the school known as mannerism, with elongated figures, compressed space, and restless light.

During the next few years, El Greco found himself preoccupied with religious commissions. He became an important member of the community, often entertaining high officials and hiring musicians to play at feasts. He filled one room of his large house with the small drawings he prepared as studies for his paintings, reserving another chamber for the statues he fashioned from clay or wax. Like many Renaissance artists, El Greco excelled in a variety of disciplines, including sculpture and architecture. Sculptures of religious figures often accompanied his paintings to form a *retablo,* a three-dimensional scene.

After about four years in Spain, El Greco finally received a commission from the king. The work he painted, *The Martyrdom of St. Maurice,* is rife with lavish color, military costumes, angels floating on clouds, and religious emotion. But King Philip did not take to the work, so it languished in the basement of the Escorial for many years until its rescue by the court painter **Diego Velazquez** (see entry) a generation later. Today it is one of the centerpieces of the Escorial.

Unique style heightens spirituality of work

El Greco may not have been favored by the king, but he received a number of commissions for religious paintings, as well as some portraits. More importantly, he created a bold and energetic style of painting, often with unusual colors and new forms, which served to heighten the emotional impact and spirituality of his works. One of the masterpieces of his religious paintings is *The Burial of the Count of Orgaz,* a large altarpiece

The Burial of the Count of Orgaz, *1586. Oil on canvas,* ▶ *approx. 16' x 12'. Santo Tomé, Toledo, Spain. Reproduced by permission of Alinari/Art Resource, NY.*

at the Church of St. Thomas in Toledo. It depicts two saints lifting the body of the count while a crowd of noblemen stand behind. Above, a scene of heaven unfolds, with angels and major figures of Christianity appearing, including Christ, the Virgin Mary, John the Baptist, St. Peter, and St. Thomas. The figures in the lower or earthly half of the painting are realistically rendered and the mood is quiet. In heaven, the light quivers, draperies swirl, and there is a feeling of spiritual tension.

In this and other paintings, El Greco's skill in representing the human hand is often noted by art historians. Like Michelangelo and others, he believed that distortion helped to express emotion and mystery. Elongated fingers, stretched bodies and faces, and broad gestures suggest a spiritual component. Such stylistic choices, though they violated accepted ideas of illustration, generally ennobled El Greco's subjects; in his portrait of *Fray Felix Hortensio Paravicino,* they helped portray a sensitive poet and scholar. Some of his contemporaries thought El Greco was either blind or mad to paint figures in this manner.

But modern viewers generally find such exaggeration for effect less jarring; indeed, it often appears distinctly modern.

Devoted career to religious commissions

El Greco spent his career meeting the constant demand for new religious works. He employed a number of assistants in his workshop, turning out paintings of saints, apostles, and religious scenes. The artist received commissions to decorate private chapels and provided altarpieces for several hospitals around Toledo.

Among El Greco's most beautiful paintings is a landscape titled *View of Toledo* or *Toledo in a Storm*. It captures storm clouds gathering in the sky above structures on a hillside and is one of the painter's few landscapes. *Toledo* features the same feeling of mystery and the tense, flickering light of El Greco's religious paintings. Many critics believe this piece inspired **Vincent van Gogh**'s (see entry) famous painting *Starry Night*.

El Greco's work was not known widely outside Toledo during his lifetime or for several centuries after his death. It was only in the early twentieth century that a German art critic, Julius Meier-Graefe, went to Spain in search of work by Velazquez and returned with an appreciation for El Greco. By this time the highly expressive art of innovators like **Pablo Picasso** (see entry) had challenged many long-held assumptions about representation; these later artists helped repopularize their more adventurous forebears. El Greco's unique, personal style links him with such contemporary masters.

Masterworks	
1577	*El Espolio (The Disrobing of Christ)*
1579	*Assumption of the Virgin*
1582	*Martyrdom of St. Maurice*
1586	*The Burial of Count Orgaz*
1600	*View of Toledo (Toledo in a Storm)*
1605	*Fray Felix Hortensio Paravicino* (portrait)
1612	*The Opening of the Fifth Seal*

Walter Gropius

Born May 18, 1883
Berlin, Germany
Died July 5, 1969
Boston, Massachusetts

"We want to create a clear, organic architecture unencumbered by lying facades and trickeries; we want an architecture adapted to our world of machines, radios and fast motor cars."

I n 1969 the *New York Times* called Walter Gropius "the Shaper of Modern Design." Through his ideas, buildings, and teaching, Gropius introduced a revolutionary concept of modern architecture and design. Structures that feature large walls of glass, prefabricated houses, recessed lighting, and sleek functional design of appliances and electronics are all part of Gropius's legacy. He became a highly respected architect and teacher by stressing two key precepts of art—beauty and function—as well as two important principles of achieving these goals—team work and social responsibility.

The Gropius family had a long tradition in the fields of painting and architecture. So it was no surprise when Walter Gropius decided early on to become an architect. His father, also named Walter, was a land surveyor in Berlin. Young Gropius attended schools in Berlin and graduated in 1903. He then began architecture studies at the Technische Hochschule (technical college) in Munich and also worked in the studio of two architecture professors there. In 1904 Gropius was forced to leave school to complete his required military training. He returned to architecture school in Berlin and in 1906 built his first project, housing for workers on a country estate owned by his uncle.

Apprenticed with industrial designer

From 1906 to 1908 Gropius spent most of his time traveling, in Spain, Italy, and England. He then returned to Berlin and became the head assistant to a well-known and respected architect, Peter Behrens. Behrens was originally a painter. But he eventually became more interested in architecture and industrial design, the design of buildings, machines, and tools for industry. He was a founder of the Deutscher Werkbund, an organization established to better standards of design and improve the factory environment for workers. Behrens influenced and encouraged Gropius, including his work in several design expositions sponsored by the Werkbund and helping him make important contacts.

Gropius maintained a private architecture firm from 1910 to 1914. During this time he designed and built several factories and residences. One of his most famous works was the Fagus-Werk (shoe factory), built with his partner Adolf Meyer. In this endeavor, Gropius employed many of the ideas he had learned from Behrens, including clean lines and minimal decoration. But perhaps more importantly, he strove to make sure the design of the structure was ideally suited to its purpose. The surprising element was Gropius's use of glass. This was the first time that large areas of glass were used as walls, the material even forming corners of the building. One architectural writer called this innovation—commonplace today—"a sudden and unexpected statement of a new [architectural] language."

Established Bauhaus

After serving in the German army during World War I, Gropius was invited to Weimar to become director of two state

schools, one of the arts and one of arts and crafts. Gropius combined the two schools into what is probably the most famous school of the arts ever founded. The formal name was the Staatliches Bauhaus, but it has generally become known as the Bauhaus. The Bauhaus was Gropius's attempt to transform arts education, to combine the technique of the craftsperson with the creativity of the artist. He wanted artists to come out of their isolation and work with designers and architects to create structures that were both beautiful and functional. Experimentation, teamwork, and real-life experience were important elements of Bauhaus curriculum. Gropius hired some of the best-known artists and craftspeople of the day and arranged for them to teach in teams—a technician and artist for each team. They offered many disciplines, including painting, furniture design, ceramics, weaving, architecture, and stage design.

Gropius was married twice during the Bauhaus years. His first wife was Alma Mahler, the former wife of composer Gustav Mahler. They were divorced in 1921. In 1923 he married Ise Franck. He had a daughter from each marriage. His first wife described him as "a gentle, sentimental person." Others found him charming and

optimistic. Gropius was also known to have tremendous drive and purpose in his work and was attentive to details of the smallest design projects as well as the largest buildings.

In 1925 the Bauhaus moved to the city of Dessau. Gropius designed the new school building, which is considered one of his finest structures. It emphasized the unity of the arts by providing large open spaces to serve as classrooms, studios, and laboratories. The design was functional, comfortable, and attractive. These were the major goals of the style Gropius and the Bauhaus developed, which became known as the International Style. The fruits of this concept of design have become so common that we hardly notice them. Today designers of everything from chairs to toasters to cars have been influenced by the ideas of the Bauhaus and the International Style. According to Ada Louise Huxtable, a prominent architecture critic, a visit to the housewares section of any department store will reveal many examples of the design ideas of Walter Gropius.

Bauhaus. Dessau, Germany, 1925-26. Photograph courtesy The Museum of Modern Art, New York.

Walter Gropius

The Bauhaus

At the end of the nineteenth century, traditional education was being criticized for its increasing irrelevance to real life. New educational methods were being proposed and experimental schools were opened. In 1919, in one of the first of the new approaches to higher education, Walter Gropius founded the Staatliches Bauhaus, or simply, the Bauhaus, as a school of design and architecture in Weimar, Germany. His aim was to encourage architects, painters, sculptors, and other artists to work together to provide the infrastructure of the modern world. He wished to train artists in the time-honored tradition of apprenticeship, in which students learn the "craft," the skills and techniques of their chosen field, from established practitioners. This training, which would enable students to most efficiently utilize their talents, was the cornerstone of the Bauhaus philosophy.

To bring his vision to fruition, Gropius hired some of the most famous and promising artists of the time. These included **Wassily Kandinsky** (see entry), Laszlo Moholy-Nagy, Paul Klee, Josef Albers, Lyonel Feininger, Marcel Breuer, and Johannes Itten. In the early years, each class was taught by two instructors, an artist and a craftsperson skilled in the same art form as the artist. Students learned to handle the materials and tools of their field, as well as the history and ideas behind it. They studied the scientific aspects of light, color, and texture, as well as ergonomics, the study of design dedicated to creating maximum efficiency and comfort. Gropius believed in education as part of the larger world; he sent students into the workplace instead of sequestering them and their professors in an "ivory tower" academic environment. He was convinced that they needed to apply their work to real life. As part of their stud-

Immigrated to United States

Gropius left the Bauhaus in 1928 to return to private business, designing many residences, shops, and apartments. He built several "settlements," or housing projects, some of which were celebrated with awards. Practicing the teamwork that he preached, he rarely worked alone, usually collaborating with a partner or group. Marcel Breuer, who had been a student and then teacher at the Bauhaus, worked with him on several projects. He also designed car bodies for the Adler Automobile Company and developed designs for the Frank Stove Factory. When the Nazis came to power in the early 1930s, they closed the

ies, they worked in a factory to witness first-hand design and production standards in actual use.

But the Bauhaus was more than just a school. It was a laboratory for many experiments in art and design. Teachers and students worked together to solve design problems and formulate ideas for improving life in the modern machine age. They rejected antiquated notions of form and beauty. Employing innovative materials and techniques, they created beauty from the function and structure of whatever they designed—chairs, lighting, windows, buildings. This new vision was called the International Style.

The Bauhaus was a small school. At its height in 1929 it had only about 200 students and fewer than 20 full- and part-time staff members. Nonetheless, its influence was enormous. Gropius's expansive views encouraged him to actively export the school's ideas and works to all parts of the world through publications, debates, and a variety of publicity. Political events also contributed to the spread of Bauhaus concepts. When the Nazis closed the school in 1933, its staff and students scattered to many areas of the world, bringing their message of the International Style with them. Gropius, Breuer, Moholy-Nagy, and architect Mies van der Rohe, to name just a few, immigrated to the United States.

Indeed, the legacy of the Bauhaus on Western culture has been incredibly broad. Architecture critic Ada Louise Huxtable attested in 1969, "Bauhaus teaching has influenced almost everything we touch." From how schools are run to what our homes and offices look like, elements of the Bauhaus philosophy are still prevalent more than 75 years after its founding.

Bauhaus and many other art schools. Artists, designers, and architects left Germany in droves. Gropius went first to England, where he collaborated with architect Maxwell Fry on some residences and a college. In the mid-1930s he relocated to the United States. He and Breuer, who had also emigrated from Germany, spent several years building houses in the Boston area. They also contributed projects to the 1939 World's Fair in New York, as well as to several colleges.

Education again became Gropius's focus when he became a professor of architecture at Harvard University in 1937. He served as the department chair from 1938 to 1952. The Harvard

Gropius House, Lincoln, Massachusetts, 1937. Photograph by Robert M. Craig.

Graduate School of Design became one of the top architectural centers in the world under Gropius. He influenced another generation of students who, like the Bauhaus students, spread the International Style around the world. Some of his pupils became leading architects, among them Paul Rudolph and Philip Johnson. During these years Gropius further developed many of his concepts of teamwork and the social responsibility of architects. He was determined that both housing and work environments serve their inhabitants. As an extension of these convictions, he became involved in city planning, writing articles and books on ways to make cities more comfortable for people.

In 1945 Gropius formed the Architects' Collaborative, a group practice for design and construction. The Collaborative worked on numerous projects, including the U.S. Embassy building in Athens, Greece, structures for Baghdad University, and the Harvard Graduate Center. Gropius's group was also the first to develop a system for prefabrication, or creating sections of buildings at disparate locations and assembling them later on a single site.

Gropius maintained an active career until his death at the age of 86. He received many awards and honorary degrees during his lifetime. His work has been featured in exhibits the world over and has appeared in numerous journals and books. The

Masterworks

Architecture

1911	Fagus-Werk (shoe factory), Alfeld-an-der Leine, Germany
1921	Adolf Sommerfeld House, Dahlem, Berlin, Germany
1925-26	Bauhaus Building, Dessau, Germany
1937	Gropius House, Lincoln, Massachusetts
1946	Impington Village School, Cambridgeshire, England
1949-50	Harvard Graduate Center, Cambridge, Massachusetts
1956	U.S. Embassy, Athens, Greece
1957	Pan American Building, New York, New York
1968	John F. Kennedy Federal Office Building, Boston, Massachusetts

Writings

1935	*The New Architecture and the Bauhaus*
1938	*Bauhaus, 1919-1928*
1945	*Rebuilding Our Communities*
1952	*Architecture and Design in the Age of Science*

year before the architect's death, the editor of *Architectural Forum* wrote that Gropius was "one of the leading architects of the century, ... the inventor of modern industrial design, ... and the most influential educator in architecture, city planning and design for the past 50 years." A legend in his own time, he nonetheless remained a model of modesty. He requested that after his death there be no mourning or funeral; instead, he wished his loved ones to hold a "fiesta à la Bauhaus" to celebrate his accomplishments. His friends and relatives met in Boston the day after his death and toasted him with champagne and deservedly lavish praise.

Duane Hanson

Born January 17, 1925
Alexandria, Minnesota

"I'm interested in the human form, and especially faces and bodies that have suffered like some weather-worn landscape the erosion of time."

n the late 1960s, when he was more than 40 years old, Duane Hanson discarded all the artworks he had made and began working in a totally new style. Using plastic resins, he created life-size models of people wearing real clothes and carrying real bags or other accessories—figures so cannily designed that at an exhibition of his work it is sometimes hard to tell the sculptures from the visitors. These recreations of undistinguished folk make a profound collective statement about the state of the American psyche.

Hanson grew up during the Great Depression on an isolated dairy farm in Minnesota run by his parents, Dewey O. Hanson and Agnes Nelson Hanson. When he was five, the family moved to Parkers Prairie, a small town near their farm. Despite hard times, Hanson—who was beset by numerous allergies—recalls that his family had enough to get by. "We had our own garden," he remembered. "My mother canned. We never bought anything at the store. My father built his house, the garage, the barn."

When he decided to become an artist, he found little career encouragement; neither Hanson's parents nor anyone they knew in this rural area of Minnesota were interested in art. The local library had one art book, which Hanson remembers poring over many times, studying prints of eighteenth-century English paintings. His first visit to an art gallery was during a trip to Minneapolis when he was 16. Wood carvings were his only creative output during these years.

Hanson graduated from high school during World War II. After being exempted from military service because of his health, he began studying at a small college in Iowa, but left after one year because of its limited art curriculum. At the University of Washington in Seattle, Hanson found encouragement from a professor who sculpted figures from logs using an axe. For his senior year, Hanson returned to Minnesota and became the first art major ever to graduate from Macalester College.

Began experimenting with plastics

Hanson began teaching art at various schools around the Midwest while working on his master's degree. In 1950 and 1951 he studied under two well-known sculptors, Bill McVey and Carl Milles, at the Cranbrook Academy of Art in Michigan. After completing his degree, he taught in Connecticut and then at several schools serving U.S. military families in Germany; he spent about seven years there. While abroad he met George Grygo, the artist who introduced him to plastics. Hanson was excited by this new medium and its natural possibilities, but he had yet to find an avenue for its use.

After returning to the United States in 1960, Hanson taught in Georgia and Florida for several years. He describes his work of the period as "abstract and decorative," as well as unsatisfying. Despite his ongoing experimentation with plastics, he felt his art career was at a standstill. "I wasn't happy with what I was doing," Hanson told a writer for *ARTnews*. "There was no attempt to communicate any deep feeling or to say anything about how I felt.... In the 1950s you were made to feel that you had to be going along with the mainstream or you wouldn't get any notice."

◀ *Portrait (p. 174): Photograph by Murray Spitzer, courtesy of Duane Hanson.*

Then, in the mid-1960s, Hanson became interested in a new, increasingly fashionable school of artistic thought: **pop art.** In large measure a rebellion against the **abstract** styles of the 1940s and 1950s, pop art employed everyday images—advertising, packaging, and even cartoons—to convey messages about modern existence. George Segal, a sculptor of about Hanson's age, was achieving renown for his white plaster sculptures of people from all walks of life; he situated these ghostly figures in bedrooms, restaurants, and other familiar locales. Thanks in part to Segal's example, Hanson literally started over, destroying all his previous work and making clay models that he then cast in polyester resin and fiberglass. He soon developed a technique of taking casts directly from live models, which lent the figures a greater realistic depiction.

Created controversy with unsettling realism

His first sculpture, from 1966, was called *Abortion*. It depicts the figure of a dead, pregnant woman covered with a sheet. "There was a lot of controversy written up in the papers about abortions in Miami," Hanson explained. "They were illegal and girls were dying. I wanted to say something about it." This was the first of many sensational figures Hanson sculpted in the next four years. These included *War,* a bloody scene of soldiers from the Vietnam war; *Accident,* a portrayal of a motorcycle crash; and *Gangland Victim,* the presentation of a mutilated corpse washed up on a beach. Local critics and much of the public were outraged by Hanson's work, which resulted in the banning of several pieces from public exhibition. Their extreme realism was simply too much. The director of a museum in Miami commented, "People come here to relax and see some beauty, not to throw up." Clearly, Hanson had struck a nerve.

Hanson's work soon began to attract attention in the New York art world. Three pieces were included in a show at the Whitney Museum of American Art in 1969. He had his first solo show at the prominent O. K. Harris Gallery in 1970. By

◀ *Hanson, left, with a life-sized, sculpted self-portrait in July 1977. Reproduced by permission of UPI/Bettmann.*

Supermarket Shopper,
1970. Polyester resin polychromed in oil, with clothing, steel cart, groceries; life-size. Reproduced by permission of Duane Hanson.

then Hanson had moved to his own studio in New York. During this period the focus of his work shifted from violence to satirical depictions of what he considered typically American characters: baton twirlers, boxers, sports figures. These pieces were not as successful as the artist had hoped; despite Hanson's attempt to invest his work with movement, he knew that much of it appeared static.

But around 1970 Hanson discovered the perfect mix of technique and expression. Sculpting average Americans—housewives, shoppers, tourists, construction workers—in reflective poses, Hanson was able to render them both humorous and sympathetic. He also managed to create a focused critique of American materialism while simultaneously suggesting Americans' frustration and want. His 1970 work *Tourists* features a loudly dressed elderly couple with all the requisite accessories: tote bag, camera, sunglasses, and sandals. Equally recognizable is the construction worker in *Hard Hat,* who sits with his can of Coke and lunchbox. His face is a portrait of worry and fatigue.

Methodical procedure produces uncanny results

Hanson selects models for his figures—usually friends or people he sees in shops or restaurants—and photographs them in various poses, attempting to familiarize himself with them so that he can put as much of their personalities as he can into the work at hand. He then makes a series of molds of parts of his subject's bodies. Each area is coated first with Vaseline and then with a fast-setting silicone rubber, which is in turn covered with reinforced plaster. This is a painstaking process, especially around the head and face. After the molds are completed, a liquid casting material, usually vinyl, is poured into each mold and allowed to harden overnight. The next day the molds are removed. Hanson uses a soldering iron to join the "seams" and correct any imperfections, smoothing the surfaces with sandpaper and files. He paints skin color with an airbrush; hand brushes are used for the additional colors defining the lips, eyes, and other more detailed elements of the figure.

Masterworks

1966	*Abortion*
1969	*War*
1970	*Hard Hat*
	Tourists
1976	*Museum Guard*
1979	*Self-Portrait with Model*
1981	*Football Player*
1983-84	*The Jogger*
1987	*Camper*
1992	*Salesman*

To complete the sculpture, Hanson at first used wigs and clothing. But when he moved from using hard plastic to softer vinyl, he found he could actually poke through the surface of the sculpture to attach fake or real hair to the scalp, face, and skin. He often obtains clothing, sometimes whole ensembles, from the models, adding yet another measure of authenticity.

Since the 1970s Hanson has created numerous figures, almost all lower- and middle-class "types": janitors, shoppers, waitresses, house painters, museum guards, the homeless. More recently he has focused on executives, students, and joggers, among others. As his technique became more sure, so did the illusion of life in his figures. Viewers flocked to his first national exhibit when it toured the United States from 1976 to 1978. At first they were drawn to the surprising and humorous aspects of the works, by the illusion of artificial "real" people. Ultimately though, few viewers were able to ignore the more serious social message. One writer concluded that the show was "a profoundly uncomfortable experience.... The exhibition finally shaped up ... as close encounters with ourselves." Indeed, Hanson's remarkable ability to render a familiar type in a typical pose enables people to recognize elements of themselves that they would perhaps rather not see. There is also an unsettling voyeuristic quality involved in experiencing Hanson's work.

Hanson's efforts have not earned universal praise; some critics have likened them to wax-museum fare, while others consider them too theatrical. But their popularity among museum visitors continues. The artist's basic figures have changed little in the decades since he began crafting them, but his intent has evolved. The satire of the 1970s gave way in the 1980s to a more compassionate view of humankind's struggles, chief among them loneliness. In the 1990s his figures seem to challenge our ideas about prejudice and social class, thus provoking further debate and achieving Hanson's ultimate aim—expressing his view of ordinary folk and making us think about our own.

David Hockney

Born July 9, 1937
Bradford, Yorkshire, England

From his early days in art school in the 1950s, David Hockney was not satisfied with the abstract style in which so many other artists were working. Indeed, his work has concentrated on very tangible subjects—friends and family, travel, life in southern California. He has captured these in painting, printmaking, and photography. Hockney has also designed sets and costumes for several operas. In recent years, his attention has turned toward the use of common technology, such as photocopiers and fax machines, in his work. Hockney's signature style is recognizable for bright colors, unusual perspectives, and a sense of humor and optimism about life. He has become one of the best-known and most popular of contemporary artists.

Hockney is the fourth of five children of Kenneth and Laura Hockney. Kenneth Hockney worked as an accountant's assistant in the industrial town of Bradford in the Yorkshire district of England. His son remembers him having an interest

"Some people have got the idea that if it's boring it's art and if it's not boring it's not art. Well, I've always thought it was the other way round. If it's boring, more than likely it's not art, if it's exciting, thrilling, more than likely it is."

in painting. They painted old bicycles together. Laura Hockney was a religious woman and strict vegetarian. David Hockney enjoyed a close relationship with his parents throughout his life and has rendered many portraits of them separately and together.

Hockney attended school in Bradford, where he was largely unhappy. "I was probably too bored," he recalls in his book *Pictures by David Hockney.* By the time he was 11, he had decided to become an artist. "The meaning of the word 'artist' to me then was very vague," he revealed. "The man who made Christmas cards was an artist, the man who painted posters was an artist.... Anyone was an artist who in his job had to pick up a brush and paint something." The lack of art classes at school greatly frustrated Hockney. As his career developed, he pursued teaching and became dedicated to art education, attesting, "Visual education is ... of vast importance because the things we see around us affect us all our lives."

Art school alleviated boredom

Hockney found it difficult to convince his parents and teachers that he was ready for art school. But finally, when he was 16 he began studies at the Bradford Art School. The curriculum relied on traditional styles of painting and design. Hockney remembers being elated to study in an environment where he enjoyed doing everything. He attended classes all day and often went to drawing classes at night as well.

He sold his first painting, *Portrait of My Father,* during his second year at school at an exhibition of local artists. He used the proceeds to buy his friends drinks in the local pub, saving the remainder for canvas and paints. It was the beginning of his climb to success.

During his last year at Bradford, Hockney began to question the accepted styles he had studied and realized that he knew nothing about modern art. He had actually never seen much art beyond a few books and small local museums. His curiosity about the breadth of artistic styles encouraged him to continue his studies. But first he was required to complete two years of military service. Hockney had been greatly influenced by the staunchly pacifist views of his father and ultimately fulfilled his commitment by working in two hospitals. He spent most of his free time reading classic literature. This was how he got his real academic education, he remembers.

In 1959 Hockney was accepted as a student in the painting department at the Royal College of Art in London. He was immediately drawn into the group of students interested in modern art, especially **abstract expressionism,** which was very popular at the time. This style focuses on the form and method of painting and is almost purely abstract, representing an emotional subject rather than a physical one. Hockney experimented with this and other abstract modes, but he was not comfortable with them. "It was too barren for me," he wrote. He continued to draw. His close friend from those days, artist R. B. Kitaj, recalled that Hockney could draw "just a little better than anyone else." As he progressed through school, teachers and friends began to realize how talented he was and began buying his drawings and prints. Previous to this, he had had so little money that in his first year he lived in a shed, using the sinks at school to wash up. Now his work began earning him a small income.

The first **etching** Hockney produced at the Royal College was called *Myself and My Heroes.* He pictured himself with American poet Walt Whitman, whom he admired for his love of nature and writings about the fellowship of humankind, and Indian political leader Mahatma Gandhi, whose ideas of peace and nonviolence were also crucial to his worldview. A few years later Hockney painted himself with another hero, Spanish artist **Pablo Picasso** (see entry). He discovered Picasso's work in his early years at art school and has studied and admired it throughout his life. "I would love to have met him, even just once," Hockney wrote in 1993. Picasso's death in 1973 was an important milestone in his life. In 1980, after several years of working in other media, Hockney was inspired to return to painting after seeing a large Picasso exhibit in New York. "It made me want just to paint," he remarked. Hockney's explorations of space and multiple points of view have been influenced by Picasso's ideas.

When Hockney was ready to graduate from the Royal College of Art, officials there would not award him a diploma because he had refused to attend any general studies classes. Only art classes interested him. He decided to create his own. The 1962 etching *Diploma* is a witty bogus document. School officials changed their minds a few weeks later, granting the resourceful student not only a diploma but a gold medal in painting, the highest honor awarded. Perhaps inspired by the gilded prize, he began wearing a gold jacket. This jacket, along with his oversize round glasses and bleached yellowish white hair, made Hockney an easily recognizable figure on the London art scene in the mid-1960s. His sense of humor and a gently mocking tone has appeared in much of his work over the years. To be sure, his "freshness" in a rather serious art world of abstract styles and intimidating critics made his works stand out. But his sense of play has also led to criticism that his work is superficial and merely charming.

Zoomed to the stratosphere

Shortly after graduation Hockney had his first solo exhibit in London and a show of prints at the Museum of Modern Art in New York. His popularity and prominence grew quickly. Writer and critic Carter Ratcliff observed, "He zoomed from art school to the stratosphere and stayed there." During the 1960s he traveled frequently—to Egypt, France, and throughout the United States. He taught at various universities in Iowa, Colorado, and California. Southern California especially enchanted Hockney. He was drawn to the quality of light there, the varied landscape, and the social scene, which was considerably more open and informal than in England. It was important to Hockney that he be able to live openly as a gay man.

His paintings of the 1960s demonstrate a fascination with water, glass, mirrors, and the play of light on surfaces. He produced many pictures of southern California swimming pools and sprinkler-drenched lawns. The style for which he has become best known developed at this time in his use of stark, vivid colors, large flat spaces, and an intense light casting clearly defined shadows. One famous painting from this period is *Portrait of an Artist (Pool with Two Figures)*. It depicts a corner of a pool with a person swim-

ming under the water; another figure stands looking over the edge. The flatness of the pool and deck surfaces contrasts greatly with the mountain landscape that recedes in the background.

Hockney was also fascinated by the modern architecture of the Los Angeles area. "Los Angeles is the only city where the buildings make you smile," he once said. He painted many views of the square modern houses with large walls of glass and open

Man Taking Shower in Beverly Hills, *1964. Acrylic on canvas, 167.3 cm x 167 cm. Tate Gallery, London/Art Resource, NY.*

185 | David Hockney

patios. He wrote, "I'd never seen houses like that!... [They] all had large comfortable chairs, fluffy carpets, striped paintings and pre-Columbian or primitive sculptures and recent three-dimensional work." One of the artist's most renowned impressions of such a house is *American Collectors (Fred and Marcia Weisman)*. Aside from his obvious delight in these sumptuous abodes, Hockney also relates a sense of barrenness or stiffness that suggests he would not be entirely comfortable living in one of them.

From L.A. to opera

Beginning in the 1970s, Hockney was asked by various opera companies to design sets for their productions. *The Rake's Progress* and *The Magic Flute* were the first two. He became intimately involved with the productions, studying the music and lyrics closely to better fit the set with his interpretations. Edward Rothstein of the *New York Times* wrote in 1992, "Some of the most indelibly potent images seen on the opera stage during the past 15 years have been created by the artist David Hockney." His love of color, texture, and the creation of space has produced large, unusual stage designs. They have been both praised as highly innovative and criticized as so grandiose that they "steal the show." In fact, Hockney has become so enamored of set design that he has installed a scale model of an opera stage in his studio, complete with a lighting system that allows him to create exactly the images he wants without having to go to the theater. He worked in this field throughout the 1980s and early 1990s.

Since the 1970s Hockney has used photography in service to his art. Though he has expressed his view that photography creates a one-eyed, square, frozen view of life, he has found it handy as a "research tool." One way in which Hockney has adapted photography to his own vision is through **photocollage.** Often using a Polaroid camera, he takes many shots of each part of a person or scene and then joins them together to create a large panorama. These often resemble the fractured style of **cubism,** which further links Hockney with Picasso. *Pearblossom Hwy. 11-18th April 1986* is one of

Hockney's best-known photocollages. This scene of a desert highway is comprised of hundreds of small photographs. It took nine days to complete the photographs and two weeks to assemble.

In 1981 Hockney traveled with critic and writer Stephen Spender to China. They toured the country for several weeks. Hockney was fascinated by the landscape and found the people

A Bigger Splash, *1967. Acrylic, 8' x 8'. Tate Gallery, London/Art Resource, NY.*

extremely engaging. He met a young artist who educated him about Chinese brush painting. After returning, Hockney and Spender published an account of their journey called *China Diary*. Spender wrote the text and Hockney added illustrations he had done during their travels.

Hockney's interest in Chinese art continued to grow. He considered the Chinese art of scrolls, or rolled-up paper, brilliant in its ability to lend a sense of movement and time as the viewer unfurled the scroll. He longed to express this dynamic in his painting. He thus produced several very long, horizontal paintings, among them *A Visit with Christopher and Dean*. This canvas is roughly 20 feet long and illuminates many qualities of his friends and their home.

Artistic applications of copies and fax

In recent years Hockney has become interested in the technology of the photocopier and facsimile machine. He was introduced to the color photocopier in the mid-1980s and immediately saw great potential for creating art. He bought several of the machines. The resulting work were not copies but complex prints made by sending the same piece of paper through the machine many times. The copier serves as a camera and printer. Hockney enjoys the speed of the process, which adds to the spontaneity of making the pieces. He calls them "home made prints."

In about 1988 Hockney began faxing paintings of sea scenes to his friends. He stretched them, made collages, reduced them, and then faxed them off over his telephone lines. He experimented frequently with the machine and over time the faxes got bigger and more complicated. In 1989 Hockney became the first artist to have a fax exhibit when he sent an entire show from Los Angeles to Sao Paolo, Brazil. He later did a fax show from L.A. to England. The gallery made the arrival of the faxes into an "event" or party, and film crews shot a record of both the sending and receiving of the pictures.

After rejecting abstract painting in his early years, Hockney's most recent paintings have become more abstract. Hockney calls them "internal landscapes." As he has suffered increasing hearing impairment in the last few years, his works have become more inwardly focused. A *New York Times* reviewer described a 1993 show of these internal landscapes, relating, "The 26 canvases [are] bubbling with bright, overlighted shapes that billow and snap back and forth in space, teeming with sprightly textures and patterns." In perhaps a natural outgrowth of his work with copiers and faxes, Hockney has also begun using computer technology to create original work.

Through these many years of experimenting with photography, office technology, and set design, Hockney has remained at heart a painter. He sees these other endeavors as side journeys that add to his knowledge and skill as a painter. Indeed, his incredible aptitude for drawing with color and his keen visual sense have been put to many uses during his career. He has maintained a youthful curiosity about people, technology, and life. And it is his enthusiasm that comes through in his art and makes his work among the most popular of our day.

Edward Hopper

Born July 22, 1882
Nyack, New York
Died May 15, 1967
New York, New York

Edward Hopper's vision of twentieth-century America is one of alienation, loneliness, and mystery. Hopper, considered one of the foremost realists of American art, has provided some of the modern era's most recognizable and disturbing images. The word *Hopperesque* brings to mind scenes of solitary people, foreboding houses, and almost unbearable tension. His work has been acclaimed for its bold and dramatic use of light and color, and for its investment of everyday scenarios with an eerie mood. Hopper—best known as a painter—also produced etchings and illustrations for magazines; yet from the early part of the century into the 1960s, he stayed true to his singular vision despite the profusion of styles in the art world.

When Hopper was born, his family lived in the home of his grandmother, Martha Smith, in a small town on the Hudson River north of New York City. He enjoyed a solid middle-class life with his parents, Elizabeth Smith Hopper and Garrett Henry Hopper, and his older sister, Marion. Garrett Hopper ran a dry-goods store. Elizabeth took charge of her children's education, sending them to a local private school and introducing them to art and the theater at an early age. Edward began to draw when he was quite young, employing a blackboard that he received as a gift at age seven as his first easel. He was often shy and became even more withdrawn when, at about 12 years of age, he grew to be six feet tall. Feeling awkward and isolated, he turned to drawing as a means of expression. His only other interest was sailing, and he spent much of his free time at the Nyack shipyards on the Hudson River; boats, water, and the seashore would appear frequently in his work henceforth.

◀ Portrait (p. 190): **Self-portrait.** *Reproduced by permission of AP/Wide World Photos.*

Studied at New York School of Art

After graduating from high school, Hopper began commuting daily to New York City to study at a school of illustration. His parents wanted him to study commercial art so that he would be able to earn a living. After a year, he transferred to the New York School of Art, where he studied for roughly five years. His teachers there were some of the best known of the day, including William Merritt Chase and Robert Henri. Many of his classmates became prominent artists as well, including George Bellows and Rockwell Kent. **Stuart Davis** (see entry) studied under Henri at the school a few years later. But none of these students would achieve the renown won by Hopper.

Hopper experimented with a variety of styles during his student years. He produced a vast array of drawings and some self-portraits in traditional, realist styles. **Realism** as an artistic style stemmed in part from the desire of artists from the mid-1850s on to shift their focus from idealized subjects—such as classical mythology—to more immediate concerns. Some, often called social realists, labored to depict struggles for political, social, and economic goals. Others sought an art that—as Hopper wrote in reference to his own quest—would manifest "the most exact transcription possible of my most intimate impressions of nature." Yet the means to realize this aim varied wildly. Hopper studied theories of realism at school and then turned them to his own purposes.

Ryder's House, 1954. Oil on canvas, 36⅛" × 50". National Museum of American Art, Washington, DC. Bequest of Henry Ward Ranger through the National Academy of Design. National Museum of American Art, Washington, DC/Art Resource, NY.

Hopper excelled at the New York School of Art, receiving several prizes and scholarships. His career expectations were doubtless high, but it would take years before he received any recognition. He spent much time in Paris between 1906 and 1910, painting steadily but experiencing little contact either with other artists or new styles. He painted outdoors around the city as often as possible and eventually fell under the sway of the **impressionist** school, especially its vibrant hues and use of dappled light.

Work selected by Jacqueline Kennedy

Hopper never again left the country after returning to the United States in 1910, but the influence of his sojourn in France stayed with him for many years. He earned a meager living as an illustrator for magazines and advertisements and continued to paint, spending several summers on the coasts of Massachusetts and Maine. There he painted scenes of coastal life, one of which, *The Sailboat,* he exhibited and sold at the famous Armory Show of 1913. It was the first time he sold a painting and the next-to-last for some 20 years. Another work from this period, *House of Squam Light,* was one of ten paintings chosen by First Lady Jacqueline Kennedy to hang in the White House in 1961.

In 1915 Hopper abandoned painting and began to work in **etching.** This medium involves engraving an image onto a metal plate, usually made of copper, after which the artist applies ink to the plate to make prints. Hopper soon mastered this difficult process, which requires careful, exacting work; each element of the image must be drawn in reverse so that it will print correctly. Hopper received considerable praise for his results. Indeed, exhibition judges who rejected his paintings often accepted his etchings, and in 1923 he won two awards from major associations of printmakers.

Hopper worked in this area for a decade, assaying the same subjects in these etchings as he would in later paintings: houses, railroads, boats, city streets, and female figures. Because etchings—unlike paintings or drawings—must be done in a studio rather than outdoors, Hopper relied on his interior landscape, his inner thoughts, for his subject matter. Such rumination no doubt contributed to the fully formed vision of the paintings to come.

During the summer of 1923, while vacationing on the coast of Massachusetts, Hopper began to paint watercolors of local scenes. He was encouraged by a friend, painter Josephine "Jo" Nivinson. They had met at the New York School of Art and saw each other occasionally during summers along the coast, discovering interests in common besides painting, including reading, theater, and poetry. When Nivinson had an exhibit of her watercolors at a museum in Brooklyn, New York, in the fall of 1923, she suggested that the museum director consider Hopper's watercolors as well. He agreed to include some of his paintings in the exhibit. Hopper's works garnered rave reviews, and the museum purchased one of them (his first sale since 1913). Hopper and Nivinson were married the next summer. They painted and traveled together throughout the United States, staying in just the sort of hotels and motels Hopper depicted in his works. Jo Hopper served as the model for several paintings.

Another watercolor show two years later, this time a solo exhibition, encouraged Hopper to resume painting in oils. He soon gave up his work as an illustrator and began to paint full time; nonetheless, his income was spotty because his slow, painstaking method only produced about three paintings a year. He and his wife lived simply in a modest apartment in New York City, escaping the city heat by summering on Cape Cod.

Developed haunting signature style

Hopper's mature style surfaced first in *House by the Railroad,* a 1925 work that has since become quite celebrated. This canvas conveys a sense of great stillness—but not calm—with its large, old Victorian house looming spookily over the railroad tracks. Menace is implied here, but never explicitly demonstrated; such was Hopper's unique ability to suggest a sinister or melancholy subtext in an apparently unremarkable scene. His use of clear, direct light, sharp color contrasts, surprising points of view, and sudden cropping of the edge of the picture all contributed to this effect. Perhaps more than anything, Hopper is known for portraying bleak, deserted locales and scenes somehow shadowed by death or other forms of loss.

Individual figures in barren hotel or apartment rooms are another typical Hopper subject. These subjects seem vulnerable and exposed, their aloneness transforming the viewer into a voyeur. *Hotel Room,* from 1931, for example, shows a woman sitting on a bed, her luggage nearby. She holds a paper, perhaps a letter, in her hand, and the angle of her head and her posture telegraph her loneliness. Another painting, *Room in New York,* presents two people in a small room. A man at the left is hunched over a newspaper, paying no attention to the woman sitting by the piano about to press one of the keys. The viewer sees this frozen scene through the window, as if from an apartment across the way or perhaps riding by on an elevated train. Although the scene lacks movement, it conveys enormous tension—the emotional distance between the two figures is tangible.

Nighthawks, *1942.*
33" x 60". The Art Institute
of Chicago. Reproduced
by permission of AP/Wide
World Photos.

These kinds of portrayals placed Hopper in a class by himself among American painters. His canvases gained wider recognition when the Museum of Modern Art in New York gave him a solo show in 1933. Critics recognized him as a unique talent and quickly understood the singularly American nature of his work. While other artists were clearly influenced by European painting even when they depicted typically American subjects, Hopper's style sprang entirely from his domestic surroundings, making him, as one critic wrote, a "true and powerful interpreter of the American scene."

Painted desolate diner of *Nighthawks*

Hopper's most famous painting, *Nighthawks,* dates from 1942. It has become a symbol of the loneliness of city life and the potential drama in an ordinary situation. The viewer looks across a barren street through the large glass window of a diner, where a man sits alone at the counter with his back to the viewer. A couple sit around the corner of the counter, facing the waiter, who reaches below. The cold, excessively bright light inside the

Masterworks

1925	*House by the Railroad*
1930	*Tables for Ladies*
1931	*Hotel Room*
1932	*Room in New York*
1939	*New York Movie*
	Cape Cod Evening
1940	*Office at Night*
1942	*Nighthawks*
1963	*Sun in an Empty Room*

diner casts a harsh glow. Once again, though nothing extraordinary seems to be occurring, the painting transmits a feeling of foreboding and melancholy. Hopper leaves the source of this mood to our imagination.

Hopper's work appeared frequently in exhibitions between the 1940s and the 1960s, achieving an unprecedented popularity. While modern styles like **abstract expressionism, color field painting,** and **pop art** developed and flourished, Hopper remained true to the mode that so eloquently communicated his distinctive perspective. In 1951 he wrote, "The only quality that endures in art is a personal vision of the world. Methods are transient: personality is enduring." Having become, as the *New York Times* put it, "one of America's most distinguished and most individualistic painters," he received a host of honors and awards. On the occasion of his death, art critic John Canaday wrote that Hopper "had distilled from the confusion of the 20th century an expression of modern America." This Hopperesque expression has influenced many aspects of the arts in America—among them writing, filmmaking, dance, theater, and even advertising.

Frida Kahlo

Born July 6, 1907
Coyoacán, Mexico
Died July 13, 1954
Coyoacán, Mexico

For nearly two decades after her death in 1954, Frida Kahlo's work was virtually unknown; she was generally identified simply as the wife of Mexican social realist painter **Diego Rivera** (see entry). Thanks to the burgeoning multiculturalism and feminism of the 1970s, however, her creations underwent a renaissance, and an admittedly somewhat idealized conception of her persona transformed her into an icon. Kahlo boldly expressed her Mexican heritage and her womanhood in her work, but she was unafraid to represent as well the physical and emotional pain with which her life was suffused. Her strength of character has become legendary in our time, spawning the "Kahlo Cult" of the 1980s and 1990s.

The house where Magdalena Carmen Frida Kahlo y Calderón was born in the early 1900s—and where she died nearly a half-century later—sat on the outskirts of Mexico City. Her parents had moved there a few years before she was born. Kahlo's father, Guillermo Kahlo—of Hungarian-Jewish descent—fled

"I paint my own reality. The only thing I know is that I paint because I need to, and I paint always whatever passes through my head."

▲ *Portrait: Reproduced by permission of Archive Photos.*

Frida Kahlo

his native Germany and arrived in Mexico when he was 19. For most of his life, Guillermo Kahlo suffered from a nerve disease that caused occasional seizures, but he managed to hold a variety of jobs during the 1890s in Mexico City. When his first wife died, he fell in love with a fellow employee at the jewelry store where he worked, Matilda Calderón y Gonzalez, daughter of a photographer of Indian descent. When Matilda and Guillermo were married, she encouraged him to take up photography like her father, and he saw considerable success in this endeavor. By the time their third daughter, Frida, was born, he had become an official photographer for the Mexican government. Until he lost his job because of the 1910 Mexican Revolution, Guillermo Kahlo provided his family, which by then included four daughters, with a comfortable life.

Rebel from the start

Frida Kahlo and her younger sister, Cristina, were sent to school together when they were three and four years old, respectively. Frida immediately became known as the school prankster. Their mother taught them the traditional skills of cooking, sewing, and cleaning but was less successful at instilling in them her deep Catholic faith. Frida and Cristina rebelled against this religious rigor and often skipped their catechism classes. Frida loved to spend time with her father, often accompanying him to a nearby park where he would paint and she would gather insects, plants, rocks, and other treasures. Her father taught her a great deal about art, photography, and archaeology. Frida frequently helped him through seizures during their outings.

When Frida was six, she was stricken with polio, a nerve and muscle disease that usually restricts muscle development. After a nine-month confinement, the disease left her right leg shorter and thinner than her left. When she recovered, the family doctor recommended plenty of exercise. Her father encouraged her in a variety of sports—including soccer, boxing, swimming, bicycling, and roller skating—despite the fact that few other girls in those days participated in them. Regardless of her energy and sports skills, neighborhood children teased her about her disability. She became outwardly very "boyish" and outspoken but remembered feeling lonely and different from the other children.

When she was 14, Kahlo began attending the National Preparatory School in Mexico City, then considered the best school in the country. The children of the most prominent families went there, and the teachers were among the top scholars of Mexico. The many political and cultural changes taking place in the country were reflected in the classes and atmosphere of the school. Especially important was the belief that European culture should be discarded and native Mexican culture appreciated and encouraged. Kahlo was among a small group of girls there and right away established a reputation as a "character," participating fully in school activities but maintaining her mischievous side.

Met Rivera at National Preparatory School

It was at the National Preparatory School that Kahlo met her future husband, Diego Rivera. He was in his thirties and already an established and somewhat famous painter. He had been commissioned by the Ministry of Education to paint murals depicting Mexican history on the walls of the school, and Kahlo regularly watched him, sometimes calling teasingly at the artist as he worked from his scaffolding.

A tragic accident changed Kahlo's life when she was 18 years old. A bus she was riding in was hit by a trolley car; she sustained massive injuries and it was feared that she would not survive. She lived, but never fully recovered. Over the next 30 years she weathered over 30 operations, mostly on her spine and right foot. She suffered constant pain and fatigue and was forced to wear a variety of braces, crutches, and other corrective devices. The lively young woman was forced to be still and thus became more withdrawn.

It was around this time that Kahlo began to paint, beginning with portraits of her family and herself. From the start, her paintings—with their clear outlines, vibrant colors, and precise details—showed intense emotion and boldness. Kahlo took her paintings to Rivera, who felt she had talent and encouraged her. They began a relationship that would last the

rest of Kahlo's life; they married in 1929, when Kahlo was 22 and Rivera 43.

Although they clearly loved each other, their relationship over the next 25 years was stormy, steeped in the intense political and cultural upheavals of their time. Rivera often caused Kahlo great unhappiness, and yet they served as spiritual and artistic supports for each other. So colorful and prominent were Rivera and Kahlo as personalities—they were the "superstar couple" of their day— that the ups and downs of their marriage often appeared in the news.

They were quite a couple: the huge, outspoken, often rumpled Rivera and the slim, attractive Kahlo, who often dressed in traditional Mexican clothes and jewelry, with yarn braided into her dark hair. During a period spent in Detroit, Michigan, while Rivera was painting his famous murals for the Detroit Institute of Arts, Kahlo was hospitalized after a miscarriage. Her pain and grief inspired several paintings, including *Childbirth* and *Henry Ford Hospital*. Like many of her works, they were rendered in oil paint on tin like traditional Mexican "votive" paintings, small works commemorating recovery from some great danger or illness hung in churches.

Work expressed psychic and physical pain

Unlike Rivera's big, public works, Kahlo's art was more personal and most of her canvases were small. Her work largely addressed her pain—both the physical agony caused by her medical problems and the anguish of her relationship with Rivera, as well as her inability to have children. Many of the almost 200 paintings she produced are self-portraits, often bloody and disturbing. *The Little Deer* depicts her as a deer in the forest with arrows puncturing her body, while others show her with a severed limb or other injuries. Yet many of her self-portraits are also beautiful, revealing her inner strength, courage, and intelligence. All of Kahlo's paintings are rife with symbols—objects representing events in her life, religion, or Mexican culture and history. In her 1938 painting *What the Water Gave Me,* she presents her legs and feet in the bath. Floating in the water are skyscrapers, skeletons, insects, and portraits of her parents.

What the Water Gave Me and other works created a link in the minds of many viewers between Kahlo and the style of **surrealism,** which was at its height in the 1930s. Kahlo had in fact met André Breton, the founder of surrealism; he admired her works and included 18 of them in a 1939 exhibition of Mexican art he organized in Paris. When Kahlo traveled to France for the show, she was entertained and praised by many prominent artists of the day, including France's **Marcel Duchamp,** Spaniard

Masterworks

1931	*Frida and Diego Rivera*
1932	*Self-Portrait on the Borderline between Mexico and the United States*
	Henry Ford Hospital
1936	*My Grandparents, My Parents and I*
1938	*What the Water Gave Me*
1939	*The Two Fridas*
1940	*Self-Portrait with Monkey*
1944	*The Broken Column*
1946	*The Little Deer*
1949	*Diego and I*

Pablo **Picasso,** and the Russian **Wassily Kandinsky** (see entries). A noted Paris fashion designer even began incorporating Kahlo's Mexican style of dress into her designs.

Political activist

In addition to socializing with the art world, Kahlo and Rivera were deeply involved with Communist politics from the 1930s on, taking part in numerous marches and protests and hosting such revolutionary figures as the Russian leader Leon Trotsky. In later life Kahlo further politicized her paintings by adding flags, slogans, and peace doves. Indeed, a few days before she died, she disobeyed her doctor's orders and joined a political demonstration in downtown Mexico City. After her death the director of Mexico's National Institute of Fine Arts was dismissed for allowing Kahlo's coffin to be draped with the Soviet flag while lying in state in the museum.

In the 1950s Kahlo's health steadily declined, and she was often confined to her bed. In April 1953, just over a year before her death, her friends organized the first major exhibition of her work in Mexico City. Not expected to attend due to her poor health, she made a dramatic entrance on the evening the show opened, arriving in an ambulance. She was carried in and placed on her four-poster bed, which had been brought in earlier. Over two hundred friends and admirers gathered around the bed and sang Mexican songs with her throughout the evening.

Kahlo died at her home in Coyoacán during the summer of 1954 at the age of 47. The residence, untouched since then, is now the Frida Kahlo Museum. In 1984 the Mexican government declared her work part of the "national patrimony," placing her among a small group of male Mexican artists, including Rivera, whose works are protected from leaving the country.

In recent years scores of writers and historians have attempted to explain the continuing appeal of Kahlo's life story and art. The preoccupation with pain in her work is understandable, but her most notable attribute, as Kahlo's biographer Hayden Herrera insisted, "is her strength in adversity." She never betrayed her artistic vision, despite living in a conservative, Eurocentric, male-dominated culture, and she never shrank from depicting her experience as a woman, a Mexican, and a rebel. Kahlo has become the subject of numerous books, films, stage pieces, and dance performances, and her works have commanded record prices. A 1990 survey in a magazine marketed to teenage girls identified Kahlo as one of 20 most-admired women of this century. After languishing in obscurity for many years, she has earned a prominent place in modern cultural history.

Wassily Kandinsky

Born December 4, 1866
Moscow, Russia
Died December 13, 1944
Neuilly-sur-Seine, France

"The horse carries the rider with strength and swiftness. But it is the rider who guides the horse. A talent will bring an artist with strength and swiftness to great heights. But it is the artist that directs his own talent."

The idea that art needn't merely reproduce external images began to gain acceptance in the second half of the nineteenth century. Wassily Kandinsky is often credited with making this concept real by creating the first totally abstract painting. From the age of 30, Kandinsky committed himself to recording his impressions of the modern age, unhindered by the demands of realism and dedicated solely to personal expression. So vastly influential is his work that virtually every stylistic development after World War II bore its imprint.

Kandinsky was raised in a prosperous Russian family, the son of a successful Moscow merchant. He studied art and piano as a child, developing a great love for music, especially opera. His parents divorced when he was about five, and his father took the children to live in Odessa, a city on the Black Sea. They spent the summers in Moscow when Kandinsky was a teenager; at 18 he moved there to attend Moscow University. The city served as a source of inspiration for much of Kandinsky's art from this period. He loved its architecture and often wrote about and attempted to capture on canvas the beauty of Moscow at dusk. He also harbored a deep fondness for church icons, religious paintings and statues, and Russian **folk art.**

At the university Kandinsky studied law and political economics. His interest in art overtook his other concerns, however, and by the time he was 30, he decided to devote himself to painting. Traveling to Munich, Germany, in 1896, he enrolled in a prestigious art school. There he befriended Franz Marc, with whom he and other students formed Phalanx, a group devoted to modern art and the first of several artist organizations Kandinsky would establish. His work during these early years was strongly influenced by a style popular in Munich called Jugendstil, or Youth Style—a mixture of medieval art, curving vegetation forms like flowers and vines, and flat areas of vivid color.

Impressionism inspired abstraction

He was also attracted to ideas borrowed from French **impressionism.** In 1895 Kandinsky had seen one of the haystack paintings of **Claude Monet** (see entry) and became fascinated by its shimmering light; he realized that the "subject" of this painting, the haystack, was less important than the effect produced by the confluence of light and color. This dramatic realization instigated the process that led him toward pure abstraction—paintings that did not "represent" a concrete subject outside of the frame.

In the early 1900s Kandinsky traveled extensively throughout Europe and North Africa with his friend and former student Gabriele Münter; he also lived in Paris for almost a year. There he became familiar with the free use of brilliant color among the **fauvists,** chief among them **Henri Matisse** (see entry). On returning to Germany he began experimenting with these artists' advances in color and form in some of his landscape paintings. *Street in Murnau* and *Study for Landscape with Tower* employ startling hues to define space and form. The landscapes serve as a link between Kandinsky's earlier traditional work and his fully abstract style. He painted some of these scenes repeatedly, each time increasing the dominance of form and color at the expense of "subject."

From 1908 to 1909 Kandinsky founded another group in Munich, the New Artists Association. Within a couple of years, however, he and several others felt the group had become too conservative, so they splintered off to form the most famous association of all, the Blaue Reiter (Blue Rider), in 1911. The new organization held two exhibits in 1912 and also published a yearbook of art to spread information about new developments on all fronts. Kandinsky and his colleagues believed in the concept of "total" art, arguing the legitimacy of all styles. Their yearbook contained works by and writings about various contemporary artists, as well as coverage of folk art, African art, and even children's art. They planned to publish an issue every year but were thwarted in this endeavor by the outbreak of World War I.

Developed greater reliance on color

The Blaue Reiter years, from about 1910 to the beginning of World War I in 1914, were very productive for Kandinsky, both in painting and writing. While living with Münter and collaborating closely with Marc, he clarified many of his ideas. His painting, meanwhile, became more dependent on color and less on specific objects or scenes. He painted what is considered the first abstract painting in 1910. **Abstract art** differs from traditional styles in that instead of attempting to represent the visible world, artists working in it depend on color and form to express their inner landscape. This mode is sometimes called non-objective, as it departs from the aim of objectively representing the material realm.

Kandinsky's 1910 work *Composition I,* or *Improvisation,* is comprised of free-form shapes of red, blue, and green joined by freely painted lines; its slashes of color lend it energy and movement. Many of the artist's works from these years have titles like *Composition, Improvisation,* or just color names, which further indicated his commitment to abstraction. Indeed, his use

Landscape with Red Spots.
Reproduced by permission of The Bettmann Archive.

of the term *improvisation,* which frequently appears in the musician's lexicon, was no coincidence; a musician himself, Kandinsky saw many common elements between visual and sonic art, likening a painted line to a musical melody and complex paintings to symphonies or jazz improvisations. And he understood implicitly that composers generally do not bother with the question "What is this concerto supposed to represent?" While working on these early abstract paintings, Kandinsky was also preparing to publish what would become a highly influential book on art theory, *Concerning the Spiritual in Art.* In making the case for abstract art, he wrote about balancing universal values with personal expression.

When World War I broke out, Kandinsky left Germany for Switzerland. He then returned to Russia, where after the Rus-

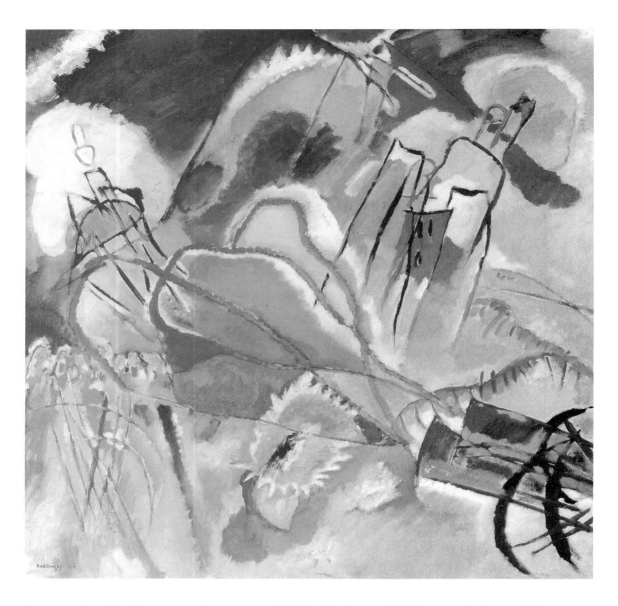

Improvisation 30 (Cannons), *oil on canvas, 1913. 109.2 cm x 109.9 cm. Arthur Jerome Eddy Memorial Collection, 1931.511. Photograph © 1994, The Art Institute of Chicago, All Rights Reserved. © 1995 Artists Rights Society (ARS), New York/ADAGP, Paris.*

sian Revolution he took an active role in reorganizing many art schools and museums; he painted very little during these years. By 1921 his art had begun to fall into disfavor with the Communist government. He returned to Germany and was invited by architect and designer **Walter Gropius** (see entry) to become a teacher at the Bauhaus, an innovative new art school. He was a member of the faculty there for about five years, teaching mostly painting theory. During this time he also published his second book, *Point and Line to Plane.*

Kandinsky sought a "language" of color and form that would express feeling in much the same way musical notes do. Kandinsky's interest in music inspired him to write two plays with musical accompaniment, *Black and White* and *The Green Sound.* He also worked on a one-act opera, *The Yellow Sound,* in which he attempted to create a total art environment, employing visual art, music, dance, and theater. *The Yellow Sound* was not produced, however, until 1982, when it served as the centerpiece of an exhibit of Kandinsky's paintings at the Guggenheim Museum in New York.

Kandinsky's art from the 1920s made greater use of geometric forms. He may have been influenced during his stay in Russia by artists working in a style known as Suprematism, as well as by Bauhaus ideas. *Yellow, Red, Blue* and *Dividing Line,* two paintings from these years, feature lines that appear to have been drawn with a straight edge rather than freehand. Nonetheless, they amply convey the energy and movement of his previous work.

Dangerous spirit

When the Nazis came to power in Germany in the early 1930s, they closed numerous art schools, including the Bauhaus. Kandinsky in particular was singled out; the director of the Bauhaus was ordered to fire him, Nazi officials insisting, "He is dangerous for us due to his spirit." The Nazis confiscated 57 of his works. Kandinsky moved to Paris and took up residence in an apartment located for him by artist **Marcel Duchamp** (see entry). He lived there for the rest of his life and became a

French citizen in 1939. Influences of the new style developing in Paris in the 1930s, **surrealism,** can be detected in Kandinsky's works from that time. Despite their persistent abstraction, some, like *Mouvement,* from 1935, utilize the wavy lines, amoeba-like forms, and intense colors favored by the surrealists. One art historian defined his work as "a wild assortment of dancing little shapes" on colorful backgrounds and called them "personal abstract fantasy." Kandinsky himself remarked, "The creation of a work of art is like the creation of a world."

One of the major collectors of Kandinsky's art during his lifetime was the wealthy American Solomon Guggenheim, founder of the Museum of Non-Objective Art in New York (later the Guggenheim Museum), the collection of which was at first mostly comprised of Kandinsky's works. Through various exhibitions and key art dealers who brought his works to the United States, Kandinsky's ideas began to influence American painters. An exhibition in the spring of 1945 in New York, a few months after Kandinsky's death, had a tremendous impact on the art world, as did many others well into the contemporary era. In the 1940s artists like Arshile Gorky and **Stuart Davis** (see entry) found great power in his works. So too did the artists **Jackson Pollock** (see entry), Hans Hoffman, Lee Krasner, and Willem de Kooning, who established the new movement called **abstract expressionism.** These artists further explored Kandinsky's conviction that art comes from within and need not refer explicitly to the physical world.

Reviewing an exhibition in the spring of 1994, a writer attested that a show of Kandinsky's art was a "vital reminder of the power of abstract painting." Along with **Pablo Picasso** (see entry) and Matisse, Kandinsky is considered one of the most influential artists of the twentieth century. Few abstract artists of the past 50 years omit his name when listing their sources of inspiration.

Käthe Kollwitz

*Born July 8, 1867
Königsberg, East Prussia
(Germany)
Died April 22, 1945
Moritzburg, Germany*

T he world has lost one of its great graphic artists and humanity one of its most valiant champions," wrote Howard Devree in the *New York Times* on the death of Käthe Kollwitz in 1945. Kollwitz's reputation derives from drawings and prints depicting the horrors of oppression, war, and injustice, though she also ventured into painting and sculpture. Whatever her medium, she strove constantly to better the condition of humanity by appealing to the empathy of viewers, consistently revealing the beauty and dignity of those who suffered.

The 78 years of Kollwitz's life spanned a period of incredible change and disruption in her native Germany. The country became an empire unified under a monarchy in 1870, went on to experience defeat in World War I, attempted to construct a democracy in the 1920s, and saw the rise of Nazism and another world war the following decade. Kollwitz was raised in a family committed to helping the less fortunate. Her grandfather and later her father headed a religious community called the

"The true reason why I began to depict only the workers' lives lies in the fact that the subjects simply and unreservedly gave me all that I considered beautiful."

Free Congregation, which stressed ethical practices and social justice. These values influenced the young Kollwitz profoundly. Her family encouraged her to study history, economics, philosophy, and literature at a time when many girls were taught only art, music, sewing, and household skills.

Developed skill in graphic arts

Kollwitz did study art as a teenager, producing drawings of local dockworkers and boatmen. She then moved to the larger cities of Berlin and Munich to study at the Women's Art Schools, since women were not admitted to the mainstream art academies. After encouragement from a teacher, she decided that drawing and printmaking best suited her artistic aspirations. She developed her skills in drawing, **etching, lithography,** and later **woodcut engraving.** Works fashioned in these "graphic" arts, as they are called, can be printed repeatedly and are less expensive to produce, thus enabling the artist to sell them at very reasonable prices.

While studying in Berlin in 1891, Kollwitz (born Käthe Schmidt) met and married Karl Kollwitz, despite her family's disapproval; they felt the marriage would interfere with her career. Their concerns were unfounded. Indeed, she continued in her artistic endeavors and began to take part in her husband's work as well. Karl Kollwitz, like his wife, was deeply committed to improving the lot of others. He ran a women's health clinic in a working-class area of Berlin. The two lived in the clinic building, where Kollwitz also had her studio.

Kollwitz came to know and counsel many of the women her husband treated, and they served as models for her works, embodying as they did the difficulties faced by poor women and their families. After her two sons were born in the 1890s, she often made motherhood her subject. Her first well-known series of prints, "A Weaver's Rebellion," was inspired by a play she attended in 1893. The stage production addressed the misery of life among weavers in Silesia, an industrial region of Germany, and reinforced what she already knew about the suffering of Berlin's less fortunate inhabitants.

Controversy over withdrawn prize enhanced stature

Outbreak, from "Peasants' War," 1903. Mixed media print, 19½" x 22¼".

When Kollwitz submitted her series about the revolt of the weavers to the Great Berlin Art Exhibit of 1898, she was awarded the gold medal. But the jury's decision was overruled by the kaiser, equivalent to an emperor, who said that art should not exaggerate the appearance of misery. This controversy earned Kollwitz a great deal of publicity, more than she could have hoped for by merely winning the medal. Over the next 15 years, critics began to write about her works, she had several exhibitions, and museums and collectors started to buy her prints. She won more prizes, including one for her second series of prints, "Peasants' War." She used the money she earned to help support her husband's clinic.

World War I had a devastating effect on Kollwitz: her elder son was killed in action during its first few months. In her shock and despair she became a committed pacifist and henceforth used her art to illustrate the horrible effects of war—especially on women and children. Having largely addressed the pain of others in her work, she now had a personal stake in the grief she depicted.

Kollwitz's style began to change. Before the war most of her drawings illustrated a scene or story and contained a definite, detailed setting. Afterward, her style became freer. She frequently jettisoned details to concentrate on the figures and faces of people, often filling the entire drawing with them. These subjects expressed sadness, tragedy, and hunger, but also dignity, love, and sometimes hope. Her bold style occasionally employed exaggeration or simplified forms for greater emotional effect. Her works—especially the woodcuts—relied on the stark contrasts of black and white, as exemplified by her third series of prints, "War," which she executed during the 1920s.

After World War I, during a brief flowering of democracy in Germany, Kollwitz became the first woman professor at the Prussian (later Berlin) Art Academy and was appointed head of the graphic arts department. She had studied and worked on sculpture in the past, but at the academy she was afforded a studio ample enough to accommodate large works, one of which was a memorial to her son. The granite sculpture, which depicted a grieving mother and father, was completed in 1932. During the 1920s, Kollwitz also designed numerous posters for international relief organizations.

Continued to expose dire social conditions

Kollwitz completed her fourth series of prints, "Proletariat," in 1925, powerfully outlining the brutal economic conditions of the period. *Bread!*—a particularly celebrated print from this series—expresses Kollwitz's sympathy for the hungry children

shown begging their mother for food, but also for the mother who has no food to give.

When the Nazis came to power in 1933, they closed numerous art schools and banned the work of hundreds of artists, including Kollwitz's. She was forced to resign from her professorship, and her works were removed from all exhibitions. She did not leave Berlin, but continued instead to protest political repression with her work; her mid-1930s series "Death" ad-

Masterworks

1897	*Weavers' Riot* (etching)
1902	*Plowman and Wife*
1925	*Bread!*
1932	*Parents* (granite)
1934	*Death Seizing a Woman* (lithograph)
1936	*Self-portrait* (bronze)
	Mother and Child (Pieta) (bronze)
1942	*Seed Corn Must Not Be Ground* (lithograph)

vanced the idea that Germany was destroying itself. She stayed in Berlin during the first years of World War II, but fled to the countryside for the last two years of her life, dying just before the war's end in 1945.

Despite interference from government officials at the onset and twilight of her career, Kollwitz's work was widely exhibited and appreciated during her life. Her technical skills were acclaimed but never exceeded in importance her humanitarian message. Whether starkly tender or horrific, her images always aimed to awaken the conscience. To be sure, few artists have addressed social concerns with such emotion, boldness, and beauty. Shortly before her death, Kollwitz wrote in her diary that even her parents asked her why she portrayed only the dark side of life. "I had no answer," she wrote. "I simply wasn't moved by anything else." The passion of her work has not faded in the decades since: a reviewer for *ARTnews* wrote of a 1988 exhibit that her work was still "so moving that one couldn't help being touched again by the humanity of Kollwitz's art."

Further Reading

Christo

Arenas, Jose F., *The Key to Renaissance Art,* Lerner, 1990.

Bracons, Jose, *The Key to Gothic Art,* Lerner, 1990.

Chase, Alice Elizabeth, *Famous Artists of the Past,* Platt & Munk, 1964.

Cirlot, Lourdes, *The Key to Modern Art of the Early Twentieth Century,* Lerner, 1990.

Cook, J., *Understanding Modern Art,* E D C Publishing, 1992.

Frayling, Christopher, Helen Frayling, and Ron van der Meer, *The Art Pack,* Knopf, 1992.

Greenberg, Jan, and Sandra Jordan, *The Painter's Eye: Learning to Look at Contemporary American Art,* Delacorte, 1991.

Greenberg, Jan, and Sandra Jordan, *The Sculptor's Eye: Looking at Contemporary American Art,* Delacorte, 1993.

Isaacson, Philip M., *A Short Walk around the Pyramids and through the World of Art,* Knopf, 1993.

Janson, H. W., and Anthony E. Janson, *History of Art for Young People,* 4th ed., Abrams, 1982.

Kennet, Frances, *Looking at Painting,* Marshall Cavendish, 1990.

Reyero, Carlos, *The Key to Art from Romanticism to Impressionism,* Lerner, 1990.

Salvi, Francesco, *The Impressionists: The Origin of Modern Painting,* Peter Bedrick Books, 1994.

Triado, Juan-Ramon, *The Key to Baroque Art,* Lerner, 1990.

Ventura, Piero, *Great Painters,* Putnam, 1984.

Woolf, Felicity, *Picture This Century: An Introduction to Twentieth-Century Art,* Doubleday, 1992.

Index

*Bolds indicate biographees
and volume numbers;
illustrations are marked by (ill.).*

Yellow Calla
by Georgia O'Keeffe

Matisse, Henri 1: 17, 22, 67-68, 97, 110, 141, 205, 210; **2: 289-295,** 343-344, 369, 421
Maximilian I (of Germany) **1:** 117-119
Mayan art **2:** 321
Mc Vey, Bill **1:** 175
Medici family **2:** 256, 297-298, 303
Meier-Graefe, Julius **1:** 165
Mellow Pad (Davis) **1:** 100
Metamorphosis of Narcissus (Dali) **1:** 91 (ill.)
Metropolitan Museum (New York) **2:** 421-422
Mexican experience **1:** 197-201; **2:** 378-387
Mexican folk art **2:** 378-379, 383, 387
Meyer, Adolf **1:** 167
Michelangelo 1: 30, 120, 160; **2: 296-303,** 390-391, 394, 435, 453
Michelangelo (Daniel de Volterra) **2:** 296 (ill.)
The Militia Company of Captain Frans Banning Cocq (*see The Night Watch*)
Milles, Carl **1:** 175
Ministry of Public Education (Mexico City) **2:** 381
Miro, Joan **1:** 92
Mitchell, Joan **1:** 124
Mobiles **1:** 34, 37-38
Modigliani, Amedeo **1:** 28; **2:** 380
Moholy-Nagy, Laszlo **1:** 38, 170-171
Mona Lisa (*see La Gioconda*)
Mondriaan, Pieter (*see* **Mondrian, Piet**)
Mondrian, Piet 1: 37, 100; **2: 304-309**
Monet, Claude 1: 50, 59-60, 138, 148, 205; **2:** 263, 277-278, **310-317,** 343, 364-366, 412
Monolith—Moon and Half Dome, Yosemite National Park, California, 1960 (Adams) **1:** 11 (ill.)
Montgomery, Alabama **2:** 268-269
Mont Sainte-Victoire (Cézanne) **1:** 61 (ill.)

Monument for Tirgui Jui (Brancusi) **1:** 27
The Moon-Woman (Pollock) **2:** 353
Moonrise, Hernandez, New Mexico, 1921 (Adams) **1:** 13 (ill.)
Moore, Demi **2:** 247
Moore, Henry 2: 318-323
Morisot, Berthe **1:** 53; **2:** 278, 314, 366
Mosaics **1:** 160-161
Moscow, Russia **1:** 69, 204-205
Mother and Infant (Cassatt) **1:** 52 (ill.)
Motherwell, Robert **1:** 127
Moulin Rouge **2:** 441-442
Mountains and Sea (Frankenthaler) **1:** 125
Mouvement (Kandinsky) **1:** 210
Mt. Rushmore, South Dakota **2:** 325
Mural (Men without Women) (Davis) **1:** 100
Museum of African Art (New York) **2:** 269-270
Museum of Contemporary Art (Chicago, Illinois) **1:** 83
Museum of Modern Art (New York) **1:** 4, 14, 20, 195
Myself and My Heroes (Hockney) **1:** 183

N

Nadar, Paul **2:** 274
The Naked Maja (Goya) **1:** 157
National Center for Atmospheric Research **2:** 338
National Gallery of Art, East Wing (Washington, D.C.; Pei) **2:** 339-340, 339 (ill.)
National Gallery of Britain **2:** 449
National Medal of Arts **1:** 22
National Portrait Gallery **2:** 248
National Preparatory School (Mexico City) **1:** 199
Nazi Party **1:** 45-46, 71, 82, 170-171, 209, 215-216; **2:** 295
Neon light **1:** 39
Netherlandish Proverbs **1:** 30
New Artists Association **1:** 206

Rudolph, Paul **1:** 172
Rue Montorgueil Decked Out with Flags (Monet) **2:** 315
Running Fence, Marin and Sonoma counties, California (Christo) **1:** 85, 86 (ill.)
Russian experience **1:** 64-73
Russian Revolution **1:** 69
Ryder's House (Hopper) **1:** 192 (ill.)

S

Sacco and Vanzetti trial **2:** 385
The Sacrament of the Last Supper (Dali) **1:** 94 (ill.)
The Sailboat (Hopper) **1:** 193
The Salon in the Rue des Moulins (Toulouse-Lautrec) **2:** 441
Salon of Contemporary Negro Art **2:** 408
San Francisco Art Institute **1:** 14
Sara in a Green Bonnet (Cassatt) **1:** 54 (ill.)
Savage, Augusta 2: 237-238, **404-410**
Savage Studio of Arts and Crafts **2:** 407-408
Schapiro, Miriam **1:** 77
Schongauer, Martin **1:** 114-115
Schwitters, Kurt **2:** 287
Scientific photography **1:** 6-7
Sculpture **2:** 394-395
Seated Nude (Moore) **2:** 320 (ill.)
Segal, George **1:** 177; **2:** 394
Seifert, Charles **2:** 238
Self-portrait at the Age of 52 (Rembrandt) **2:** 357 (ill.)
Self-portrait (Cézanne) **1:** 57 (ill.)
Self-portrait (Davis) **1:** 96 (ill.)
Self-portrait (Dürer) **1:** 113 (ill.)
Self-portrait (Gauguin) **1:** 137 (ill.)
Self-portrait (van Gogh) **1:** 144 (ill.)
Self-portrait (Goya) **1:** 152 (ill.)
Self-portrait (El Greco) **1:** 158 (ill.)
Self-portrait (Hanson) **1:** 176 (ill.)
Self-portrait (Hopper) **1:** 190 (ill.)
Self-portrait (Kollwitz) **1:** 211 (ill.)
Self-portrait (Leonardo) **2:** 250 (ill.)

Self-portrait (Lichtenstein) **2:** 264
Self-portrait (Rubens) **2:** 397 (ill.)
Self-portrait (Velazquez) **2:** 451 (ill.)
Self-portrait with Seven Fingers (Chagall) **1:** 64 (ill.)
Senghor, Leopold Sedar **1:** 17
Seurat, Georges 1: 148; **2:** 346, **411-417**
"The Seven Deadly Sins" (Bruegel) **1:** 30
Sexism **1:** 75-76
Shahn, Ben **2:** 385
Shchukin, Sergei **2:** 292
"Shelter Drawings" (Moore) **2:** 321
Shoah **1:** 80
Shoffer, Nicolas **1:** 39
Sierra Club **1:** 10, 13
Signac, Paul **2:** 413
Sinking Sun (Lichtenstein) **2:** 261-262
Siqueiros, David Alfaro **2:** 352, 382
Sisley, Alfred **2:** 311-314, 365-366
Sistine Chapel **2:** 302-303
Sluyters, Jan **2:** 305
Smith, David **1:** 123
Snowstorm: Steamer off a Harbour's Mouth (Turner) **2:** 446 (ill.), 447
Soak-stain technique **1:** 122, 124-127
Social realism **2:** 384-385
Soft Watches (*see The Persistence of Memory*)
Solarization **2:** 284
Solomon R. Guggenheim Museum (New York; Wright) **1:** 209-210; **2:** 473 (ill.)
Southern California **1:** 184-185
South Pacific **1:** 142-143
Spanish Civil War **2:** 348
Spender, Stephen **1:** 187-188
Spiral Group **1:** 19-20
Spoleto, Italy **1:** 83
Springer, Roselle **1:** 100
Stabiles **1:** 34, 37-41
The Starry Night (van Gogh) **1:** 149 (ill.), 151